CW00498687

Are We There Yet?

A personal journey on both sides of healthcare

Dearest
Jan + Mark
Enjoy, lots of Love,
Jules
xx.

JULIANA SAMSON

Contents

I dedicate this book to Dad

with Love

"You held my hand for a while,

but you hold my heart forever"

Introduction

The inspiration for this book came from an experience that I had, on learning that my Dad was diagnosed with a type of Leukaemia that has a 10-year mortality. I was 10 years into my career as a physiotherapist at the time, so this news gave pause to reflect on how fast the past 10 years had flown by, and to question where I wanted to be in the next 10.

Or more importantly, who I wanted to be. The experience challenged me to show up as the best version of myself, in all my life roles. As a student, clinician, boss and an employee. As a daughter, sister, wife and step mum.

I take you through my journey of learning from life. At times I manage successfully, and at times with much vulnerability. None of these roles or lessons are separate from one another. My lessons from relationships with family and friends; shaped my values as a professional and as a human - because of this, the journey may resonate with parts of yours.

Our fears, insecurities, intentions and motivations may be shared. I hope my story connects with your experience on either or both sides of healthcare.

Chapter 1

The graduate journey

I remember all too well what it was like becoming a new grad. I recall my physiotherapy registration certificate landing in the post and on opening it, feeling this huge surge of relief and happiness. The kind that comes with getting something I've wanted and worked towards for so long. Then I remember the fear. The kind that comes with realising that I finally have what I wanted and also the responsibility that goes with the title. There I sat with this certificate in hand, stomach churning. I have recognition as a Physiotherapist by the governing body - as of today, I thought. Yesterday I knew no more than I do today, yet here I am today. My mind was telling me I wasn't ready.

For my induction, I was walking through the corridors of one of the biggest teaching hospitals in Sydney alongside the head of the Physiotherapy Department. When asked, 'Which rotation would you prefer first?' I replied with something like, 'Anything except intensive care or nights please, as I feel that my clinical placement in ICU was limited.' More to the point, I believed that spending half a day *observing* in ICU on one student rotation, gave me virtually zip experience. I had it in my head, that if I were let loose on my own in either ICU or the night shift, I'd likely kill someone. I mustn't have given off that impression though - (I can do 'outwardly cool' really well by the way), because I later learned that the department head allocated the more responsible posts to those that seemed most mature and capable at induction. She granted me my wish and kept me away from the dreaded ICU or night shift... for week one that is. She rostered me for nights at week 2 instead!

I had a week of day shifts, covering areas that were short staffed, and then alternate weeks were night shifts. I spent one evening with a senior on the first night and then I would have a telephone number for support for the rest of the time. 'Phone a friend,' like on the TV game show 'Who wants to be a Millionaire' wasn't the start to my career that I had in mind. I was terrified. 'Somebody's definitely going to die,' I told my boyfriend at home. He reassured me that this system wouldn't ˙ be in place if new grads ended up killing people off as a result. He was right. It was just one of many times in my career when

I realised that, although diving into what I thought was the deep end, I learned that I wasn't in over my head after all. My training provided me with more than I thought I had, and there was loads of support around, not just from senior physiotherapists, but from the entire hospital team. Those times when I've stepped into the abyss terrified, have been my greatest periods of learning.

What I was less equipped to deal with, was the emotional side of the job. Night shift saw me treating the most poorly patients in the hospital on my own. Those who wouldn't last the night or would deteriorate overnight without treatment were on my list, alongside emergencies that arrived. I remember one evening crying in the back stairwell before seeing this lady who was on 'comfort measures'. Basically, my suctioning treatment, which (despite my best efforts) would be uncomfortable, would clear her airways enough to ease the work of breathing and prolong her life perhaps for a few more hours or days. I was 23 years of age, sobbing alone in the stairwell at the thought of doing this. Then I checked in a mirror to be sure that it didn't look like I'd been crying, before I entered the ward to introduce myself to the family and ask if they would mind stepping out whilst I treated their mum.

I still remember clearly, 2 patients in that year who died when they were initially expected to make a full recovery. I remember the hours away from work that I spent searching my mind for answers. Could we have done more? Could I have done more? Fortunately, I worked in a time and a system that was to a high standard and after much soul searching the answer each time was no.

It was a massive culture shock from working in a major city teaching hospital with all the facilities and specialist teams, to my 3-month rural secondment, which in comparison was third world. I spent even more hours in my room in the hospital accommodation, thinking on how unfair it was that our rural cousins received substandard care compared with city folks. I worked doubly hard to make up for this and spent even more time questioning myself as to whether I could have done more or should have known more. I remember being on the phone to Olivia, my sister, feeling frustrated and a long way from home. She saved more doubts when she said the words, 'This is not your fault. It's not you.'

Initially fear was my motivator for learning. I'd better learn fast, so as not to 'kill someone,' so as to 'look competent,' to give my patients, 'what they deserve.' In the early days, I really felt like I didn't deserve the 'undivided attention' look that patients gave me each time I spoke. They were looking to me for advice and whilst outwardly I gave it with every confidence and conviction, inside I felt that I was just making it up. 'Fake it till you make it,' we used to joke amongst colleagues behind closed doors.

I remember feeling absolutely in awe, the first time I witnessed a handover of the night shift. The graduate physios from the year before, rattled off the cases. '37-year-old female multi-trauma from an MVA (motor vehicle accident) with a fractured L5, right pelvic rami and femur…. Intubated and ventilated…' and so on…. It was like they were on an episode of ER! Us newbies just stared on wide eyed. Fast forward one year on, when the graduates were watching me handover - all in a day's work. They stared at us with that same expression. Had I faked it and made it yet? There was plenty of stepping into the abyss to come.

In 2002, I was on a working holiday in the UK. I was offered a lone post in a rural Army base in Scotland by my locum agency. At this point I had only 6 months outpatient experience in Oz and 6 months in the UK. One senior therapist commented that I was, 'a bit junior for the role.' This cut deep because I felt the same way. I was aware that I probably only got the offer, because of the shortage of experienced physios at the time. The guy I was dating told me to, 'Ignore her, she's only jealous.' Then as only a soldier can, he gave me my marching orders. Echoing this, another colleague said, 'Go for it – we're on the end of a military line if you need any support.'

So, despite my fear, I went for it. I spent Christmas in Oz before starting that role and I took time out to go to the library. I copied chapters from any decent musculoskeletal resource I could find. I walked into that camp in Scotland, again terrified but covering it well. I learnt fast and worked super hard.

One day I confided in one of the nurses that I trusted. I shared that my last senior remarked that I was too junior and I feared she may have had a point. He just smiled and replied, 'You're here and you're it. You know the most out of us. We look to you and it's your call.' Just like my first stretch experience, I discovered that I knew more than I thought I knew.

I thought that someday when I knew more, my confidence would improve, but each learning just opened more stuff that I didn't know. I wanted to know it all *right now*. Over time, I realised that the push to pedal fast, motivated by fear as a driver, ultimately didn't prove anything or bring out the best in anyone. I study just as much now and definitely more effectively. I now search out of curiosity rather than fear. My patients drive me to seek answers and I'm okay with admitting if I don't know something and will get back them. On a constant learning curve, I will never know it all now, or ever. All there is to know changes anyway.

After years of suffering the pain of feeling out of my comfort zone, I grew to welcome and seek that feeling out; because it means that I'm growing. I seek out my weaknesses, not to punish myself, or out of fear, but out of a genuine desire to grow and keep growing - because I love being a physiotherapist and I love the journey. I'm now comfortable with the 'undivided attention' look from my patients and if they're not giving me this look, I ask myself whether there's a communication issue.

I used to think that this change in my outlook arrived when I gained more clinical experience and knowledge, which in turn made me more confident. This was in part true. My post graduate study in 2004 improved my assessment structure, provided more treatment skills and improved my clinical reasoning. If I knew that the course at University of South Australia in Adelaide would be that tough, I wouldn't have done it, so I'm glad I didn't know. It was one of those experiences that so radically changed the way I process cases, that I can't think of what I did before then.

The head of department, Dr Mark Jones was a physio, a psychologist and a world expert in clinical reasoning. He taught us to see the, *person* with the problem' and not just, 'treat the *problem*.' We learned the skills to assess and treat, not just the biomedical, but also the psychosocial contexts. This was reinforced by Dr David Butler's fantastic work in chronic pain. He was ahead of his time in urging us to consider the psychological, neurological and immune components of the pain experience. He was such a dynamic lecturer, with an energetic style. We always looked forward to his tutorials for both the great content and entertainment.

One of the other stars on the programme was Professor Karen Grimmer. She was a physio and an epidemiologist, meaning that she understands the bigger picture of research design and execution. Her insights about some of the issues with the current direction of physio research, were enlightening. I remember my friend from Zimbabwe sat next to me remarking, 'After all my years of physio, this is what I travelled the world to hear.'

I was lucky enough to land a position editing for one of Professor Grimmer's PhD students. It funded my study, but more importantly, I learned so much about qualitative research through the process. Saravana was the best boss ever. We started our editing sessions every Saturday by picking up a takeaway coffee at the best barista in town.

I made some dear friends there too. We were in the same tough boat together. One of my classmates made me laugh, when he said, 'I wake up every day and tell myself, I'm still a physio and they can't take that away from me.' No chance of faking it in that environment. For anyone suffering with impostor syndrome (the fear of being 'found out' or 'exposed'), this course was their worst nightmare. Our practice was examined, questioned, pulled apart and put back together. We even had to do the practical exam treatment techniques on the tutors!

Outside the practical exam rooms, the tension was often palpable. To make light of it all, and to show off to Tessa, Nathan challenged her to a high kick competition. As his competitive spirit got the better of him, he let rip on the most spectacular kick, which took his hamstring by surprise and landed him on the floor in agony. Don't expect sympathy from a bunch of physios for showing off. We all burst out laughing. As Tessa applied his leg in a stretch position, she said jokingly, 'That'll teach you to mess with Tess.' As if that wasn't funny enough, in the very next moment, his name was called into the exam room.

Tessa was my running buddy. Not being able to afford the expense and the loss of brain cells by partying, running was my main stress relief. Tessa and I covered so many hours hitting the pavements and putting the world to right. One time we went out with the intention of 'just a short one' and got so lost in conversation that we lost our sense of direction. I suspected something was wrong when the street names were German sounding. The German settlements were out towards the Adelaide hills! Thankfully we had enough cash on us to catch the 20km bus ride back into town.

The clinical reasoning process drilled into us from that course, has since allowed me to systematically eliminate possibilities if a patient fails to improve, rather than simply thinking that it was because I wasn't good enough to fix them. Through clinical reasoning, I learned to look at my own thinking processes more objectively, a process called metacognition.

In one of my first post graduate lectures, Dr Mark Jones covered the attributes of an expert, which included inquisitiveness, self-confidence, open mindedness, flexibility, honesty, diligence, reasonableness empathy and humility [5]. I remember feeling truly inspired to live this out, but I had to lose the self-criticism before I could become more self-confident, and yet more humble. It wasn't until I lost the fear of looking less than perfect and had acceptance and compassion for my human limitations; that I could truly start to grow.

"True humility is not thinking less of yourself;

it is thinking of yourself less"

C.S. Lewis.

Chapter 2
Romance in Scotland

Back in Scotland, I was the only female apart from reception and the Salvation Army welfare ladies on camp. Everyone was falling over to look after 'Jules,' the 24-year-old Aussie physio. Everyone that was except Sam; who insisted on calling me Juliana. Without having rehab instructors and gym facilities on site, I asked the fitness instructors whether they would assist in my patients' return to fitness. They were all too happy to help, but their boss Sam, politely declined my request. His team were tasked to look after mainstream fitness, not injury. Knowing what I know now, I realise that I was overstepping in my request, but I didn't mind the way he said no with those beautiful blue eyes.

There was an instant attraction between us, although at first, we both denied it, instead becoming inseparable best friends. I felt like I had known him for years and could tell him anything. Before realising it, I was spending most evenings hanging in his dorm, just chilling and chatting, sometimes into the early hours of the morning.

I popped into his block one morning for my usual coffee catch up and Sam asked what I was up to today. 'The doc wants to go to Inverness, and I would join him, but I've just realised that it's St Patrick's this weekend. I don't want to miss it in case I'm back home by next year.' The last thing that I expected was, 'See if you can book a couple of flights to Dublin and we'll go.'

It was crazy fun. Aussies aren't used to hopping on a plane and popping across to another country. As we walked to the terminal at Edinburgh, with our passports, a toothbrush and a change of pants, I said to Sam, 'This is the furthest I've travelled for a night out to the pub.' The whole trip just fell into place. The taxi took us to a hotel near town and we shopped for a change of clothes before finding the best pub ever, complete with Irish bands and families singing along. The street parades were amazing. I loved this guy's spontaneity!

On a team night out the following week, all the guys were up for a dance, except Sam, who was playing it cool at the side of the dancefloor. 'C'mon Sam,' I shouted over the music, 'Come dance with us.' 'No,' he replied. 'Aw C'mon, don't be a party pooper,' I teased, pulling his arm. He pulled me close to him and said, 'I only dance with people I sleep with,' and with those cheeky blue eyes fixed on mine, he said, 'C'mon, come to bed with me.' I could have jumped him there and then, but I knew that he was in Scotland on a trial separation during this 6-month post. Although it sounded as though the marriage had long finished and she called for the separation, I was wary of getting involved in case there was any chance they could reunite. Their daughter Sarah was just 6 years of age at the time and I had no plans to stay in the UK. I didn't even know where in the UK the next locum job would take me in 3 month's time.

Soon after, Sam was returning home to visit his family in Yorkshire, and I said before he set off, 'You should try to get back together,' speaking from my head and not my heart. 'Why?' he asked. 'Because ending a family's a big deal.' 'Of course, I know it is,' he replied, 'but if she can get to a place to end it once, she'll do it again.' They agreed to separate for good that weekend and so I allowed myself to fall in love with him.

After Scotland, I managed to line up a job in Yorkshire and we found a flat together. I remember speaking to Mum on the phone and she asked, 'So… things are pretty serious between you and Sam?' 'Yeah, they are,' I replied, biting my lip. 'Are you planning to stay there?' 'Yeah, I am Mum.' Silence. 'Well….' she said finally with a sad voice, 'I'll miss you.'

Having settled into our apartment, Sarah was due to visit for the weekend. I suggested that for the first few visits, I should stay in the Mess on barracks. Her parents had been separated for 6 months but Sarah had only learned about it recently. I didn't want the child to be hit with too much news. I insisted that I be introduced as Daddy's friend rather than his girlfriend. I needn't have worried though, because at her age, all are seen as friends regardless of gender.

We met in a café in town and apart from the odd translation issue with my accent, things flowed perfectly. Sarah said, 'Don't worry about your accent. We have a teacher at school called Mr Baxter. He's from Australia and he talks funny too.' Sam and I cracked up laughing. 'It would be fun to have another girl with us for the weekend. Daddy, can Jules stay over our place tonight?' I stayed on the sofa, which Sarah's mum thought was crazy. She thought that we should just come out with it, but I wanted to give her a chance to get used to things in her own time.

When it came around to our first Christmas together, I caught a bit of resistance, as Sarah began to understand that we were a couple. She didn't want to decorate the tree because it wasn't hers. 'I've known Daddy longer than you have,' she pointed out. 'Aw Sarah, this is your place and your tree as much as it is ours and yes, he's your Daddy and you've known him all your life. I would never step in the way of that.' We hadn't the time or the need to revisit this issue, as I was due to fly for my study in Adelaide in January and Sarah got in touch with how much she would miss me. She gave me one of her favourite soft toys to keep me company on the journey. 'Can't you come home?' Sarah pleaded on the phone a few weeks into my trip. 'I would love to sweetie, but I have things I need to finish here.' 'Please, just for the weekend Jules?' My heart melted.

I knew that Sarah had accepted us as a couple when Sam told me that after one phone call, he found her jumping about punching the air and cheering, 'Yes! Yes!' 'What are you so happy about?' Sam asked. 'You said you love her,' Sarah replied. 'Yeah, I always say I love her.' 'No,' Sarah returned quickly and with a smile, 'This time you said you Luuuuuv her.'

When I returned from Adelaide, Sam and I couldn't wait to get married. I had developed a close friendship with Claire, Sam's eldest daughter. She lived a crazy life as a young adult and so was getting her training done now as an OPD (Operating Department Practitioner). Despite settling down a bit, it wouldn't be a party without her and her fella, Mark. Sarah and Claire made gorgeous bridesmaids and only those in the wedding party knew what we were up to. Everyone else was invited to a housewarming. Our guests were in casual gear, with no presents, fuss or speeches. Just an Aussie style BBQ in the company of our close friends and family in the UK.

During the party, one of our neighbours assumed that Sarah lived with us, and I heard her correct them. 'I live with my mum and visit here on weekends.' They awkwardly replied, 'You must be so lucky to have two houses.' Later that evening I picked up on that interaction as an opportunity to check in on how she was doing. 'Wasn't it weird, how that neighbour said you were lucky for having 2 houses?' 'Yeah,' she replied, 'I think some people don't know what to say.' 'How *are* you doing living in 2 houses anyway?' Sarah explained how much she missed Dad coming home to a cup of tea in his big green mug, while Mum asked him how his day was, 'but it was just like a house that looked good on the outside.' She would sometimes hear muffled talk and then the front door would close and a car drive away. 'Besides,' she continued, 'had none of this happened, I would never have met you.'

One of my neighbours, Cath, had a Rottweiler cross Collie named Rooney, who needed regular runs out whilst her husband was posted to Iraq. Cath wasn't a runner at the time, so I was all too happy to step in as Roonie's running buddy. I joked that I had a part time dog and a part time daughter; but in all honesty, there was nothing part time about my love for Sarah. We had a very close bond and I became the person who she turned to when she had something that she wanted to share; with someone who wasn't mum, dad or her peers. On the weekends that Sarah stopped over, she shared her joys, fears and sorrows. I held her in my arms when she cried her broken little heart out over a best friend who had to move away, or a boy who had ended young love.

When Sam and I married, Sarah and I had a chat about what we should call me. Did step mum sound too formal? We agreed to keep on with Jules, so it was much to my surprise that I received a Mother's Day present one year. The week before, Sarah was poorly. I happened to have the day off, so at my suggestion she was dropped around to ours. I loved looking after Sarah and wanted to be ill in her place. Sam asked Sarah, 'Why have you bought her a present? She's not your mum.' 'She's like a mummy,' Sarah replied. I never felt the need to have children of my own, from having the opportunity to love and nurture on that level. Although I'm still working on Sam to consider getting a dog! As Sarah grew up, we enjoyed trips to day spas, art galleries and European cities. We even got tickets to a swimming final at the London 2012 Paralympics.

Meanwhile, Claire and Mark were busy bringing the babies into the family. Little Sammy arrived in 2007 and Sarah in 2008. When my mum would ask was, 'I going to give her grandkids,' I would joke, 'You have 2 and I have 2, so fair is fair.' Though there was no way I was being called grandma at this tender age. Jules will work again.

Chapter 3
Olivia's wedding

'Jules, can you make it in February to be my bridesmaid?' she asked. 'I wouldn't miss it for the world hun!' Olivia, my sister was marrying Erin, the loveliest guy you could ever meet. I was so pleased for her, because her last guy of 10 years was a commitment phobe to the extreme. Erin couldn't be any more different. He absolutely adored her and after a couple of years, they were ready to tie the knot.

In no time I had booked our flights to Sydney and the countdown began. It had been 3 years since my last trip, and the first time that Sam could come with; so it would be a lovely occasion to meet my Australian family. Olivia and Erin offered up their spare room so that we could get a chance to enjoy some quality time together.

A week prior to the trip (and on Valentine's day no less), Sam was searching about the house for his wedding ring. 'I took it off during my weights session and haven't seen it since. Have you moved it?' he asked. 'No honey,' I replied, 'but we had better get a temporary replacement before you meet my family or people will talk,' I laughed. 'While we're at it, we may as well get you to the barbers and make you a little more presentable,' I teased. I loved his scruff order locks, which he grew halfway down his neck. As he was no longer a soldier, he could rebel against the establishment, but I was thinking of the wedding pics for my sister.

'Make it look as though I haven't had a haircut,' he said to the barber. We're not sure how that translated into lopping all his locks off... 'I look like a dork,' he said. Sam didn't want anyone to see him before we flew out that afternoon; so I couldn't resist when I bumped into his best friend Don. Sam hid in the car as I fetched some last-minute travel supplies. I was crying with laughter as I pointed him out to Don, saying, 'Look at his head!' I'm not sure Sam has ever forgiven me. After Don was done pointing and laughing, we made our way to the airport.

I fly really well when Sam's by my side, as I feel safe to sleep away, but I make for poor company. I slept virtually all the way across the world, bar mealtimes. I've always been happiest sleeping or eating and am great at both. Sam on the other hand, sees food as merely as a fuel source and is a super light sleeper, especially on a flight. So, when we landed into Sydney and I remarked, 'Are we here already?', Sam just shook his head in amusement.

We're so opposite in so many ways. Sam grew up in rural Scotland and is a mountaineer by trade. He's fine on his own, doing extreme survival and navigating by the stars. When we met, I was a city girl and a social butterfly. My idea of navigation and survival was to have spare cash and the card of the hotel securely on my person, so that I could always get a taxi back from a night out with my friends. He's Mr chilled and cool under pressure, taking nothing personally and I was Mrs chaos, Mrs sensitive at times, who took everything personally.

Though without realising it, through a combination of growing up and living in another country, I had already begun to change my outlook. Aussie culture and particularly my family's culture are so much more laid back, whereas British and especially the military culture are far more structured. I had also set up a private practice which I ran part time, and so having an appointment-based schedule and a small business required that I learned to become more organised.

I sent out a Facebook message to my friends 4 weeks before our trip to ask them to keep time in the first week of Feb free. I was berating myself for not sending it sooner to give them more notice, until all 10 of them replied back, 'Just message us when you get here.' I forgot that Aussies woke up each day without a plan. In the UK, this would be considered crisis management, but in Oz, nothing's a crisis.

This was only a small matter, compared to how much I had changed in the family dynamic. Until this trip, I hadn't appreciated how much I was a people pleaser in my past life. Olivia could just snap her fingers and her doting sister would be at her disposal. I guess I had learned from an early age, to be agreeable and sensitive to the needs (and whims) of others. This gained affection and praise.

Olivia's praise was sparing amongst a stream of criticisms about my figure, my dress sense and personality. I didn't detect this, as it had always been this way and by being put down, I looked up to her. That was until I moved away and formed a life of my own on the other side of the globe. In the last 3 years, I became more self-assured and happier in my own skin, so when Olivia dished out the standard put downs and demands,

I wasn't ready to accept it. Stressed also by the pending wedding arrangements; my lack of placating response, seemed to escalate her behaviour to the level of all out tantrums.

She screeched at Sam at the top of her lungs to, 'EAT SOMETHING!' as the growing atmosphere put him off grabbing a snack from the kitchen before going out. I couldn't blame the guy for losing his appetite and wanting to escape.

Lindsay, one of my closest primary school friends, met us in the bar and when we shared the story, she asked, 'So did you eat something?' 'Hell no', laughed Sam, 'we don't indulge spoiled children.' I chimed in with my story, where Olivia said at the dressmakers, 'This dress will suit you, as it's fit for more curvy figures.' I laughed, but Lindsay looked kind of shocked. She covered it quickly; laughing along and saying sarcastically, 'Yeah, 'cause you're just sooo massive.'

I'm a size 10, but I always felt big and awkward as a young adult. Olivia's childhood pet names for me didn't help. Horse ankles, childbearing hips, clumsy clutz were some of her favourites. I think it's possible looking back, I that I might be

25

mildly dyspraxic. At 1 metre 67cm, I'm the tallest of the women in my immediate family.

Mum was from the Philippines, as was Olivia's and Seth's father. My dad met Mum on holidays abroad and on migrating the family to Australia, he embraced them both as his own. It was never a secret that Olivia and Seth had a different dad, yet I felt that they were as much my family as my younger brother Alex was.

There I was as a bridesmaid, with a role to serve, which I would have performed so naturally in the past. Sadly, for the situation now, our positions had changed. From me being the little girl who would do anything for the big sister that she idolised, to being my own person – not just a thing or a servant. Her shock and mounting disappointment, that I wasn't playing the expected doormat role, was creating strain. For the sake of the situation, I decided to play the subservient role this one trip, to restore family peace and so she could have her big day without conflict.

It was a surprise to me, that playing the part of someone who I've actually outgrown, was so difficult. I found myself wanting to stand up for that subservient person. I felt sadness for that inner child, who knew no different to being mistreated. I decided to stay off alcohol in Olivia's company, to ensure I refrained from saying something that I would regret. The wedding venue was in the Hunter Valley, located 2 hours north of Sydney. It was a stunning location, famous for its world class wines; so I was making a major sacrifice.

When we arrived in the Hunter, we caught up with Mum, Dad and the boys. As Seth lived in Melbourne and his daughter Paige lived with her mum, this was only the second opportunity for me to see my sweet little niece. She would have been too young to remember the first. 'How old are you now Paige?' I asked. 'I'm 6 Auntie Jules,' she replied, rolling her eyes, 'I wore a badge all day yesterday.' 'That's me told!', I laughed. Paige was such a bright, happy clever little girl with a quick wit. I wasted no time getting quality fun time in.

We all stayed in this super high-end accommodation on a nearby winery, which was arranged by Olivia for guests on our side of the family. Unfortunately, because of lack of consultation, all but my immediate family chose alternative, more affordable options. Seth and I we were left with the extra cost as we were the only ones who could (kind of) afford to cover it.

On the morning of the big day, I was taking a moment to plug into a guided mediation at the hairdressers. I took my earphones out as the hairdresser approached. 'How would you like your hair done?' By this time, I was broken. 'Whatever she wants, whatever you think,' I replied flatly. The hairdresser who had probably seen this before commented, 'Olivia thinks she's not stressed, but she is.' 'Yeah', I sighed. Paige was holding up really well, for hanging with us adults. I found myself laughing at her impression of a leapfrog, when Olivia entered the salon at that moment to say, 'Paige, don't jump out your curls darling.' My step mum nurturing instinct kicked in at that moment and I found my mission of the day. To entertain and comfort Paige.

Later in Olivia's accommodation, we were getting dressed, when Olivia came out with the most spectacular outburst. With her bridal gown on, she felt the need to have her arms moisturised. So, with them outstretched, she screeched out to no one in particular, in the most dramatic fashion, 'NIVEA!! I NEED NIVEA. NIVEAAAAA!!'. I just stood there in disbelief, as two of her friends came running to her aid. One on each arm, applying this middle of the market brand moisturiser, without so much as a thank you from their diva master. Since I moved abroad, she's managed to find herself a new supply of minions, I thought – Nivea for Queen Olivia. How funny, that just a few short years ago, I looked up to this woman and now I just thought she was kinda sad.

I felt like an actor for the entire ceremony, putting on my best attempt at a genuine smile for the photographs and all the guests. When it came time for dinner, I was seated next to Olivia and I thought on how unfortunate this situation was. When she planned this table arrangement, and I booked my trip, we were the best of friends. We holidayed through Europe for 5 weeks together for our last catch up. I'm sure we both looked forward to another close, connecting, special time, yet it turned out so differently. Perhaps it was ok for Olivia though, as she wrapped her arm around me saying, 'It's been such a wonderful day,' sharing her intention that this trip was a holiday for me too. I just smiled over the sadness.

It was Dad's turn for the father of the bride speech. The night before, Seth, Alex and I were talking among others and the subject of walking Olivia down the aisle came up. I learned that day, during the rehearsal, that she had chosen to walk unaccompanied, but clearly this hadn't been communicated to Dad. He was under the impression that he would have the honour, so I had to break the news to him. He looked disappointed, but quickly recovered and despite this, gave the most wonderful, heartfelt speech that night.

As Sam and I were happy to look out for Paige during the reception, Seth was on a mission to let his hair down. 'This is a joke and I'm getting my money's worth,' he said, as he downed another drink. He turned to Alex who was tasked with video filming duties and said, 'There's always someone in a wedding who's going to be an arse.' He looked into the camera, pointing at his own face, and said with a slur, 'tonight it's gonna be me!' My cousin Paul who is normally the comedian of the family, chimed in with, 'Well, at least it's not me for a change.' Mum gave Seth a stern motherly warning look, as Sam and I just laughed on.

As the party livened up, Mum and Dad were ready to turn it in, so it was handy that I chose to be sober. I could drive us back to our accommodation instead of ordering a taxi for them. Sam was ready to join us too, and it was reaching past Paige's bedtime. Seth wanted to stay out longer and on saying that I was happy to take Paige back and tuck her in, he said, 'I'm not normally like this, you must think I'm such a bad parent.' 'Seth, relax,' I affirmed, 'Have fun. You have a rare chance to. Besides, I'm loving being Auntie Jules today.' Bonding with Paige provided the opportunity for Seth and I to heal some very difficult things in our past, that after some deep work, I could never condone, but was able to forgive.

As I was packing, Alex came to connect at the 11th hour. I thought that he may have picked up on the weird dynamic between Olivia and I. However well hidden, Alex is very sensitive to such things and would have found it easier to stay away. I had no desire for him to be involved or take sides, so I kept the conversation away from that issue. Instead, I just stopped my packing - that could be done early hours next morning - and I enjoyed a few precious moments with him.

I must admit that for this trip, it was a relief to get on the plane and back to my life in the UK. I reflected on the flight how Sarah might have felt, going from our relatively chilled home to a more organised disciplined version with her mum and stepdad.

People have such different values, I thought. Shaped by their infinitely diverse sets of influences. It's as if people form completely different working maps of the world.

I used to feel bad for Sarah having to transit between the different realities, until I read an article that stated that those who are rigid in their organisation miss creative opportunities and those on the creative end can lack the structure to finish projects. It's probably also a good skill to learn early in life, that people have these different maps and that each one contains valuable and valid perspectives.

Family interactions were icy with Sam at times during this trip, presumably because his map was so different. Also, because my map had been updated, the family dynamic had changed. Sam shared on the plane that he had a distinct feeling at times, that my family blamed him for how I had changed, as if he was somehow controlling me. The truth couldn't be more opposite. It was precisely because of the freedom in our relationship, that I had changed, not into someone else, but into me.

Chapter 4

Dad's health

One weekend in 2010 stood out in my mind. I received a call from my parents, 'Hi Jules,' Mum began, 'we have some news and we don't want you to worry. Dad has leukaemia, but it's a very slow type. They only found it by chance on his latest diabetes check.' I couldn't process the information. Mum's casual tone of voice conveyed the message as if Dad had a sniffle or a hangover. Dad chimed in at that point. 'It's called CLL and it doesn't need treatment because the doctor said it would take years to show signs.' 'Yeah', Mum continued, 'Doc said that his drinking is likely to get him first!' followed by laughter from them both. 'So, we just wanted you to hear it from us and that there's nothing to worry about.' 'Uh, ok…' I replied, still not quite ready to laugh along. I guess they've had more time to get used this between test results and they may have been expecting worse news.

After the call, I researched online for CLL and no matter which journal I read, they all pointed to a homogeneous path of a 10-year mortality from the time of diagnosis.

10 years.

I thought on how fast the last 10 years had gone. It felt like a heartbeat since my graduation in 2000. In the next heartbeat, I'll be turning 43 and could be looking back on my Dad's life. I would remember the man that taught me to stick my principles above all else. To take a stand for integrity, truth and fairness. To find true north on the moral compass and never deviate from that. Always steadfast, honest, loyal and kind. He embodied the act of service above self in all his relationships. I have aspired to follow his example and have come a long way in 10 years, but still fall short more often than I would like to admit. Where will I be with this in a decade? Will my life be an example of the lessons of his legacy? I resolved to do better right here and then.

The first and probably best self-development book that I've ever read was '7 Habits of Highly Effective People' by Stephen Covey [2]. He covers the importance of aligning values with principles. These principles are natural laws, are timeless and felt very familiar to me, as they echoed the stand that my father taught me to take. The other useful concept from the book which made a huge impression on me, was that none of us are victims of any circumstance. That we can choose our mood and attitude in any situation. No one can make you feel anything without your consent. Whilst we aren't in control of what happens, we are in control of how we respond to it. As the saying goes,

"We cannot direct the wind, but we can adjust the sails."

Once I got my head around Dad's diagnosis, I exercised that freedom to choose to see things differently. 10 years is ample time to be grateful for, with plenty of opportunities to show up as my best and most loving self. From this reflection I resolved to take responsibility for how I view my experiences and create as many quality moments as possible. Taking nothing for granted, not only with my loved ones, but as often as I can in my life.

Not long after that first shock, my folks phoned and shared that Dad had been diagnosed with an enlarged prostate. They were waiting on a biopsy which just landed, confirming cancer. He'd been booked to see a consultant in six weeks to discuss whether they'll be operating. Once I took a moment to absorb the news, I looked at flights and phoned them. 'I can come in six weeks,' I began, or 'I can wait until you're in for treatment and visit in hospital.' Dad preferred me to come in six weeks because, 'I'd rather see you and enjoy your company while I'm well.'

I tell my UK friends that Aussie kids soon learn to stop asking, 'Are we there yet?' after they bore themselves with the answer being 'No' so often. A drive to my grandparent's took 7 hours and that's still in the same state of NSW! I guess it's made me pretty good at flying, but I admit that the map screen with that plane, illustrating the route, does get to me - especially at the start of a journey. I get it already. 6736 miles to Singapore. Grrr. After trying not to look at the stupid plane on the map screen for 24 hours, I landed into Sydney first thing in the morning.

I stopped at my Uncle Colin and Auntie Thel's, a couple of hours up the coast by train. My aim was to stay awake all day and sleep at theirs overnight. With a combination of coffee, red wine, snacks and cousins visiting all day, I was entertained in a wonderful kitchen party. Aunty Thel, grew up in the UK and so knew all too well how that flight across the world felt. She did a fantastic job of keeping me fuelled, not least with stories of her former UK life. It was also precious to spend time with my Uncle Col. We went through albums of old photos and he told me things about Grandad that I never knew. I knew that Pop was a shearer and worked on the farms. That he boxed at amateur level, but I had no idea that he competed on the national stage. Col was an athlete himself. His best half marathon time put mine to shame and at 70, he completed a long-distance cycle ride in the same time as when he was 40! Col and Sam had a real affinity when they met at Olivia's wedding. The kind of connection that 'tough guys' have when they recognise one of their own and it needs no words. I was in 'trouble' with Uncle Col for not bringing Sam along this time.

Mum and Dad phoned to let us know how it went with the consultant. They were not best pleased; least because of his poor bedside manner. One of the things that the consultant said, or at least they heard, was that it may not be worth treating the prostate at all, as he would likely die of the leukaemia sooner. Mum wanted to grab the guy from the scuff of the neck and

37

drag him across the table for, 'just killing my husband off like that.' Dad interrupted at this point to say that it could have been the language barrier. He's Spanish. The consultant had planned to order another biopsy because the previous report didn't give them enough localised data to make a decision on operating. We were all understandably upset about this. For me it was mainly the fact that there was still no plan, but another wait for a repeat investigation.

En route through Sydney, I was able to catch up with Olivia and Erin to meet their new little man, Jimmy. Contact had been sparse and things still frosty since the wedding. Olivia is a sucker for flowers, so I bought an impressive bunch and this seemed to break the ice. Jimmy was 3 months old and like my connection with Paige, children have a way of healing things. I felt such closeness holding this beautiful little boy in my arms. Something that as an Aunty, I had never expected to feel. 'Do you want a break from holding Jim so that you can get into your lunch?' offered Erin. 'No thanks,' I said beaming, 'I ordered a risotto, so that I could eat with one hand.'

Before I flew up to Queensland, I also popped into Sydney to catch up with some old school friends. Talia was a radiotherapist, and on hearing Dad's story, suggested that I get a second opinion, or at least exercise our right to request his notes. 'You have a legal right, as they're his notes,' she informed, 'but I would take the softly-softly approach and appeal to the fact that you're only in the country for short time and your parents are confused about what's going on.' Alice pointed to Joeanne, an Army medic and said, 'Of course the other way to do it, is to just kick the door down like Jo would.' We all laughed as Jo said, 'That works too!' I agreed to maybe try Talia's approach first. Talia explained that her concern was that the prostate could be a secondary to the leukaemia. She's had the experience a number of times where people have been sent from rural areas to their unit in Sydney, far later than they should have been and by that time it was too late.

After Dinner, I raced for the airport. I think through nervous energy from worry, cramming too much in and rushing around with luggage unacclimatised to the heat, I made myself ill. I arrived at my parent's house and crashed out for 2 days to rehydrate and rest. In that time my body forced me to slow down, but my brain wouldn't. I managed to speak with Dad about how he wanted to proceed. He wasn't keen for a second opinion at this stage, but he wanted more clear information. So, I submitted a request to the hospital for his medical records. To check that it had been received and get a rough time on processing, I phoned the department. The lady confirmed receipt of the application, but wasn't committing to a timeline, instead informing that she would do her best. Legally she had 10 days to supply it and I only had 5 left, so I tactfully mentioned this to her. I could hear the frustration in her voice on repeating that, 'I will do my best.' I then changed strategy to empathising with her, 'Thank you I really appreciate that, because I'm sure you must be really busy.' To this she sounded more open and sighed in reply, 'You have no idea.' 'Sorry to hear that,' I responded, 'and once again I'm really grateful…' I allowed my voice to tremble. It wasn't difficult to let tears flow, 'because the difficulty is that my folks really don't understand what's happening with Dad's cancer and we're really afraid.'

One hour later we received a phone back from the hospital to say that a meeting was available tomorrow with the cancer nurse practitioner, to go over the notes. In preparation, I pulled an all-night study session that would have rivalled my university days; learning more about prostate cancer than any physio would ever expect to. So, prepared with as much information and caffeine as I could handle, Dad and I went to the hospital. We met Judith, who explained that more often than not, prostate cancer is a slow-moving condition and although cancer sounds scary, planning treatment isn't something you'd want to rush into. 'You need to weigh the potential complications of treatment against the risk of the condition developing problems,' she said, 'Low risk prostate cancer often may never give you problems in your lifetime.' With this, Dad nodded in understanding and relief. Having indicated that he had the reassurance that he needed, Judith turned to me to answer my clinical what ifs. Dad was happy to sit back when she offered us seat by the computer and paper notes. She walked me through the notes and printed off the pathology and clinic reports to complete the file. I wondered what it must have been like for Dad to watch the discussion between two colleagues, having never seen his daughter in this professional context. By the end of the meeting we had a full set of notes and plenty of reading material for me to wade through on the plane.

I was also conscious to make this a special time with my family and so in addition to time out together, I spent one-to-one time with each. Shopping with Mum, having a beer out with Dad and skating with Alex - but I left the half pipe tricks to him. It was time to fly back home before I knew, but we had a wonderful time and also understood Dad's medical plan.

Mum and Dad hugged me as we parted at the airport and Dad said to me quietly, 'Thank you so much for what you've done, because before that we were in the dark.' As I walked through customs, I thought on what an awful place it must have been for my parents to be. I resolved that that for the rest of my career I would be an advocate for my patients and do everything I can to ensure that they are never in the dark.

On the flight back, I read through his notes and I realised that 6 months had passed between the first blood result and urology hospital appointment and a then further 6 before the biopsy result. I thought on how much worry my parents must have gone through. Then this recent consultation added to confuse matters. I took in the last thing my Dad said to me and how much impact what I'd done might have on them. It certainly had an impact on me. I was cross about this time to diagnosis, but more thanks to good luck than good management, the plan would not have changed. We had information that the cancer was contained, low-grade and without spread. We can afford to wait for the second biopsy and because of this, I didn't feel that it was helpful to point out my issues with the hospital delay to Dad, who just needed to stay positive. Instead I took lessons from the experience into my professional life.

Chapter 5

Taking a career stand

Steve Jobs' graduation speech at Stanford University from 2005 was played over in the news as a tribute to his life when he passed away on the 6th Oct 2011

The part that stuck out in my mind was:

"When I was 17, I read a quote that went something like: 'If you live each day as if it was your last, someday you'll most certainly be right.' It made an impression on me, and since then, for the past 33 years, I have looked in the mirror every morning and asked myself: 'If today were the last day of my life, would I want to do what I am about to do today?' And whenever the answer has been 'No' for too many days in a row, I know I need to change something."

http://news.stanford.edu/news/2005/june15/jobs-061505.html

It touched me to the point of welling up. I needed to change something about my current employed role. I found myself increasingly unhappy with the shrinking time allocated to patients. Whilst I appreciated that there is no such thing as a perfect system, I was struggling to reconcile the differences in the level of care that I provided in my public service role, versus my private clinic. In the morning I might be screening out for stress fractures in a recruit and in the absence of these, negotiating the shortest possible time to get back to training. Later that same day I would be taking the time with my private patients to do my very best to prepare their return to sport in a way that was robust and sustainable. There was a failsafe for the recruits that allowed them to join slow stream rehab if they failed to keep up in training, but even then, it was way more mass production than private care.

This dissonance reminded me of the time that I rotated through my rural placement in my graduate year. Having come from a big team in a major city teaching hospital, to a much smaller outfit in rural Queensland, I felt disappointed by the lack of resources and specialist skills. Burns, abdominal surgery and vascular patients would each have a separate ward, medical / surgical teams and physios in the city. In the country, all cases were combined in one surgical ward, looked after by one team and their physio - me. I remember phoning up the burns specialist physio in Sydney to ask her whether a particular dressing that was routinely used there, should be used with one of my patients up North. She was surprised to hear that it wasn't being used. I was even more surprised when the staff in the rural team hadn't even heard of it, let alone had a budget for it.

I felt that it was unfair. It would keep me awake at night - the injustice of it; that they deserved better. Likely never having lived in a city, my patients lacked the perspective of comparison that I did. I looked around and my colleagues seemed happy, content and balanced. They left on the dot at finish time - there was life outside of work. I felt alone and constrained by a system that either didn't know or care about how much better things could and should be. I would work doubly hard as if it were my responsibility to make up for it.

Given that I was only 6 months qualified at the time, I was also insecure about my own skills and so drove myself even harder. Perhaps also to escape facing my own lack of skills, my energy was focussed out rather than within. By focussing on the negative aspects of the system and projecting the faults of others, I was wearing myself out. With no downtime, pushing harder, starting early and staying back late. I was ill for a time and worked through, what I realise now was a pretty serious chest infection, that took ages to clear. In being full of resentment towards my colleagues and the system, this response inevitably failed to bring my best self forward. I maintained that I had high standards and that no one else measured up to these, when all the while I was actually falling short of my potential by allowing this negativity to dominate my focus.

It might be that my contented rural colleagues had no recent point of comparison to be dissatisfied over, but it's more likely that they understood that inequity of access to resources and skills is endemic in rural healthcare. However, this was something that they could do nothing about. They perhaps realised that they could, as Theodore Roosevelt put it,

"Do the best you can with what you have, where you are."

Unlike me, they accepted that there is no such thing as a perfect system but decided to be the best that they could within it.

I didn't want to make the same mistake again. I was determined to avoid that place of cynicism and resentment, but the problem as I saw it at the time, was that as my rehab interest developed, my awareness of how much more I couldn't deliver grew. At the same time, due to funding cuts and changes to governance structures, our influence was shrinking. I decided to discuss my feelings with my boss, 'I see my influence shrinking and shrinking and I question what impact I have anymore.' 'You do have an impact,' she replied. 'Just go to a pass off parade to see all the faces. You influence people's careers.' 'I do get that, and I've tried to flower it up, only to eventually come back to this one issue. I had been telling myself over and over, 'Just do what you can - work within your circle of influence Jules.' I'd relied on mantras such as, "At least it's not the NHS," but those words eventually sounded hollow. I could talk myself around for shorter and shorter lengths of time,' I continued, 'before I come back to the same issue. I think that things changed for me since my last trip to Oz. Dealing with Dad's mortality. Seeing the impact of him being mismanaged and asking the question of what it is to be a professional. I'm asking myself serious questions like: 'is this job in keeping with my principles?'

I had the luxury of making a choice to leave that role and needed to make that leap of faith into private practice in any case. I reflect now though, that despite my influence reducing due to circumstances, it was my focus that was the problem. I was still looking at what I couldn't do rather than what I could. For example, If I had looked at the role more as an opportunity to educate the recruits, on the importance of looking after their musculoskeletal health to prevent chronicity or to build in resilience strategies, time constraints would have been less of a concern. Perhaps not all would have taken the message, but like an educator once told me, it's not for the many that you do it, but the few.

Taking that leap of faith started the most exciting journey of my career so far. I started a practice in a room above a running shop, where from my experience with soldiers and a captive audience of people buying running kit downstairs, I soon built a reputation around specialising in running performance. Runners are such a cool group to work with. Rarely is their day-day function limited. The problem is at mile 9 of a half marathon, or running fast, or up hills. With a race coming up, the sessions are naturally goal and time oriented. The staff in the shop, all runners of course, were high on endorphins and so the place was mad crazy with personalities.

One of my runners had a complex spinal diagnosis and wanted to carry on with her marathon training, so I accompanied her during a consult with her musculoskeletal Doc. Dr Martyn Speight is a very respected and talented clinician. Unlike Oz, his specialty is more of a rarity and fights for recognition in the UK. So especially in Yorkshire, these musculoskeletal Docs are few and far between. Being an athlete himself, he understood this lady's motivation and was willing to support her training, advising on how to proceed safely. I was most impressed with his skills, but even more than that, his bedside manner. He had good rapport and empathy with my lady yet retained his straight talking Yorkshire style, carrying it off with personality.

Soon after this session, Andy, an excellent podiatry colleague, mentioned that Martyn was setting up a new centre near Leeds and had an opening for a physio. If I was interested in joining them, he would put in a good word in for me. Dr Speight remembered me right away, saying that anyone who took enough interest to attend a session with a patient was evidence enough for him. Soon after taking on a day a week in his clinic, I realised how much I missed the support of being in a strong team and how much easier my life was as a result.

After seeing enough common movement patterns in my runners, I got to asking myself, whether these patterns could precede the injury, and could there be a way to screen for this? It would be great to catch these problems before they manifested. It seems I wasn't the only one thinking this way. At the time, a big name in movement education had commenced a venture that was looking at prevention.

After attending some of their seminars, I was most impressed with the European director, Bruce, who seemed to be the conceptual force behind the approach. He had a remarkable ability to see and grasp meaningful connections between concepts that others missed. As a synthesiser myself, I could appreciate the way he was able to create something that was greater than the sum of its parts.

After going out of my way to impress Bruce and the UK director, Saskia; I was invited to join their training team. The deal was that I earned my stripes contributing to the development, marketing and user training of a running specific screen. Then on passing their exams, I would earn paid work on my own courses.

Saskia had a real skill as a coach. She could distil the complex, into clear concise lessons. She always checked that her class was keeping up with her and students would get the experience by doing and feeling. With Bruce, you got the impression that he was super clever, with Saskia, you went away thinking, 'I get it.' She taught me to be less of an out-front lecturer and more of a coach in my rehab and teaching.

As I gained a deeper grasp of their concepts, I could better keep up with Bruce and he would challenge me with as much information as I could handle; teaching me to think and problem solve for myself. Saskia seemed the driving force of the business. She was a typical entrepreneurial type. With relentless drive and capacity for work, she managed to create a presence for their product in the market. One downside of this, was that Saskia expected the same level of commitment from her team. In response, I soon embraced workaholism, allowing her to demand more and more of my personal time.

Another downside was that in all of Saskia's striving, there was a tendency to overreach, resulting in a disorganised business culture of firefighting. All of this made for a stressful working environment at times. Thankfully Bruce, with his laid-back style, brought some balance and was able to moderate when team members felt overworked and underappreciated.

I learned so much from that company, both clinically and professionally, but I also gained a glimpse of what the worst side of corporate life might look like. Typing up work in planes, trains and hotels. Breakfast, lunch and dinner meetings. Work hard, play hard and squeeze in too few gym sessions to make up for it.

I was star struck and naïve, so I took their promises on face value. I invested crazy amounts of time and effort, funding these tasks at my own expense. Head office was in Scotland and one of the courses was in Sweden! I funded myself through two of their modules at Keele University, located almost 150 miles from home.

On chatting with one of the students on the second module, she suggested that I enrol in Keele's MSc programme, 'You'll already have 45 credits,' she urged. At first, I dismissed the idea, but I think there was still some sense of incompletion from Adelaide. I had originally intended to complete their MSc, but time and circumstances called me to re-evaluate and I completed with a Grad Cert. After letting it simmer, I eventually decided to call enrolments to sound out the idea. Before I knew it, the admissions officer said, 'There you go, I've updated your file and you're on the programme.' Oops. Even then, I thought I'd just take it one module at a time and see how it goes.

To my surprise, I actually really enjoyed the change from clinical practice and the business stuff. I got better at scrutinising research and thinking for myself. It was the best update and complement to Professor Karen Grimmer's lessons in Adelaide. In a time when practice is becoming more influenced by guidelines that aren't always informed by quality research; it's more important than ever, that practitioners can discern quality and appropriate evidence for themselves.

My commitments soon crowded out much of our home life and both practices were building too. Sam had to complain on more than one occasion, that I, 'treat this house like a hotel,' before I realised that something had to give. Still seduced by the promise of a global teaching role, I considered leaving my Leeds practice. I was torn, because I enjoyed being part of Martyn's strong clinical team. When I explained this to Saskia, she replied, 'You're part of our team.' I decided, very reluctantly, to let go of my clinic in Leeds. Martyn, understood and gave his blessing, 'You've got to go for it Jules, or you'll never know.'

Chapter 6
Back to Dad

The folks phoned to share the good news. The 2nd biopsy came back negative, so the consultant cancelled surgical plans and decided to monitor his bloods for now. 'That's great,' I said, trying to hide my confusion and urge to research the specificity and sensitivity of prostate biopsies the minute I hung up.

By chance, during the time of my research, our insurance guy was reviewing our policies. On updating my family history, I disclosed Dad's recent illness. He related that he had just recovered from Prostate cancer himself. His biopsy was a 4+3 and he had the top guy in London remove it with robotic surgery. 'My Dad's first biopsy was a 3+4,' I related. '3+4!' he exclaimed. '4+3 is more serious but 3+4 is still up there. You might want a second opinion.'

I learned through my journal research, that the use of PSA blood tests and biopsies carries a high margin of error. Blood test findings can rise with benign prostate or infection. Biopsies often miss or underestimate the extent of cancer, because of the size of the small core samples compared with the whole prostate. I learned of Multiparametric MRI technology, which gives a much more accurate visualisation than standard MRI. There was a trial being run in Brisbane with the only machine in the country; so I contacted the unit. Unfortunately, the fact that Dad already had biopsies, meant that he failed to meet the inclusion criteria, but it was worth booking a consult with their top guy.

With a bit of persuasion… ok… emotional blackmail tactics, my Dad finally relented and allowed me to arrange for him to fly to Brisbane for the consult. The consultant arranged a MP-MRI scan and concluded that there was a low risk of cancer cells, and if present, is likely the low risk type.

When I updated family on this news, Alex emailed the loveliest response.

'Jules, you're incredible, I know you probably think you're just doing what you can or feel obliged to help… but I dunno what we'd do without you. I've just dealt with the feeling of helplessness and not knowing what to do and you're on the other side of the planet taking care of the situation.

Thanks too for the info, Love ya .

I replied that I'm glad to be of help and that being so far away, I feel helpless sometimes too.

That reprieve was short lived. As I parked outside the clinic just weeks later, a text from Mum landed. 'Hi Jules, will you call me when you can, it's about dad x.' My heart skipped a beat and without a damn for the cost, I phoned her right away. Dad had had a massive bowel bleed and needed a total blood transfusion. He was in ICU in Rockhampton. 'Are you okay Jules?' Mum asked after a long silence. 'No.' I replied honestly between sobs. 'I'm so sorry darling,' she said. 'It's okay,' I replied once I'd collected myself. 'Mum, I have to go to work right now, but I'll call you when I get home. Love you.'

Thanks to having experience at this, I wiped my tears, checked myself in the rear-view mirror and walked into the clinic. I sat in place just staring into space trying to collect my thoughts at first. My colleague Catherine entered to set up her room, ranting on about how annoying it was the internet went down at home this morning. 'I've got a good one for you,' I said in a calm but flat voice, 'My dad's in ICU.' 'I'm so sorry Jules,' Catherine turned her attention to me. 'I don't even know what I'm doing here. I should be there....' 'You can't be there this second,' she said gently, 'so you might as well be here and keep busy for now. I have the number of a good travel agent.' 'Thanks Catherine.'

This snapped me out of my trance. I phoned Sam, 'Honey I have some bad news about Dad and I'm keeping my head above the emotion and keeping it brief. I have a patient arriving in a few minutes. Dad is in ICU, he's had a full blood transfusion from a bowel bleed and that's all I know for now.' 'Ok,' he replied. 'What can I do to help?' 'Please can you search for flights and I'll do the same between patients.' 'No worries, love you.' That's what I love about military types, the pragmatic nature when the situation calls for it. Just like healthcare practitioners. By lunchtime we had booked me a flight leaving the next day.

Thankfully, this was the last clinic before London Marathon. So it was a simple matter of pre-race tune up treatments, complete with talk about race strategy and some positive reassurance thrown in for good measure. This was a busy clinic and provided the perfect way to keep my mind off the situation with my family. I managed to hold it together so well, almost too well in fact. I felt quite numb when talking about it when I got home. The emotion hit when I spoke to Mum.

I've never seen her like that. Virtually hysterical with crying. She was so overwhelmed that her arms were flying about when she spoke. 'I know that he has to go sometime, but not now,' she cried. My heart cried with her when she described the indignity of how Dad stumbled from losing so much blood from his rear end on a trip to the bathroom, that he started to pass out. When Mum managed to catch him, all he could say to her and the nurse was, 'Sorry.' He kept apologising for the trouble and the mess, 'You know how kind and proud he is.'

Mum passed on the details of the hospital contact for me to call. ICU picked up and then transferred me to Dad's gastroenterologist. His first question was, 'You're medical right?' I said yes. 'You're in the UK?' 'Yes.' 'It is bad. It's definitely cancer.' Bloody hell, I thought. I said I was medical, not made of rock! 'It will have to come out because of the bleeding and biopsied for staging.' Sam told me afterwards that the Doc had to repeat himself three times before I finally replied, 'Yes, I understand.'

When I stopped off in Singapore, I learned that they were unable to control the bleeding and so transferred him via the flying doctors to Brisbane. I spoke with **Alex** on Skype who agreed that Mum was really distressed. 'She even needed help booking a flight. In the end it was just easier for me to do it. She should be there in a couple of days and I'm driving up from Sydney.' As I was already touching down in Brisbane, all I had to do was find my ongoing travel to the Royal Brisbane and Women's Hospital. With time looming to re-board, combined with jetlag and emotional exhaustion, I didn't even try getting my head around the whole route. I took down the address and nearest train station. I'd probably catch a cab from there anyway.

I eventually arrived at Bowen Hills Railway Station and here wasn't a cab in sight - great. My phone didn't have global roaming back in the day, so I just picked a random direction and walked up the road on the lookout for a taxi. Dragging my trolley luggage in the blazing heat, again. Thankfully a taxi soon picked me up and there I was, transported to a hospital reception desk, asking to locate my father. 'Ward 8B, bed 5,' the helpful receptionist gave me directions. I hadn't even realised that she said *Ward* not *ICU* until I saw Dad sitting up in bed smiling at me with those green eyes. 'What are you doing here?' he said. I returned his huge smile, hardly containing my sense of joy and surprise, 'I heard weather is good here this time of year', I replied, giving him a massive hug.

He'd been nil by mouth for days and the nurses had just given him the green light to eat. 'I could eat a horse and chase the rider,' there was that cheeky smile again. The nurses supplied a wheelchair, explaining that he might be a bit anaemic. It was such fun being just him and me. I wheeled him downstairs and got to spoil him, buying whatever he wanted to eat in the café. Although this earned a mock 'tut-tut' from the nurse who took his bloods on return to the ward. 'The Kranski sausage must've pushed his blood sugar over,' I replied trying to stifle a laugh. Dad was pulling a, 'we got busted' face.

I had self-recriminations related to not pushing Dad to pursue the colonoscopy or enquiring on his behalf. When Dad first mentioned that he had bleeding and was on waitlist for a scan, Sam suggested that I should leave it to him. I saw his point; I was asking about his health every time we spoke, and it was taking the shape of a clinical history rather than conversations as his daughter. At the time, it seemed like a reasonable thing to do, but now with this outcome, is seemed like the dumbest idea in the world. I do know though as a clinician, the danger of looking back on a decision with hindsight. Decisions can only be made with the information and level of insight at the time. To be honest, I hadn't even noticed how many months had passed whilst turning my attention away from medicalising Dad. I projected my anger at Rockhampton. Knowing his history, how could they allow 6 months to pass?

My Uncle Colin echoed my sentiments. When I repeated this to Dad, he simply said that the waiting time is what comes with being under Medicare. 'It's only fair as others must have had more convincing presentations than me.' I was truly moved and humbled by that response. Living out his belief in fairness and equity; uncompromising in his principles, even when his health and maybe his life is on the line. It completely threw me. Perhaps it was to change the subject or put a lighter note on things, that Dad then shared the following story:

The team were doing their rounds and they all of stood around Dad's bed to discuss his case. There was hardly any standing room for all the people. The junior doctors and students were trying to make themselves look small and seemed uncomfortable. So to break the ice, Dad said to them all with open arms, 'Welcome to my humble abode!' The place cracked up with laughter. I laughed and cried at the same time on hearing this story. I'm so lucky to know this special man, let alone have him as my father. His empathy and capacity to put the needs of others above his own was remarkable. His grace and humour through the whole experience was truly inspiring.

Mum arrived the next day and over coffee we discussed the situation, prior to meeting Dad with his consultant. Brisbane Royal and Women's had been a brilliant and efficient team. Since arriving, he'd had consults with discharge planning, Colorectal, Radiotherapy and Oncology. He had an MRI to visualise the tumour and a contrast CT chest / abdo / pelvis to check for spread. We were now waiting on results and a plan. 'Right now, I have no news,' Mum said, 'so I have no worries and if it's bad news I'll still not worry.' The consultant explained that there was no spread of the cancer and so the plan was to remove the tumour and follow this up with 6 weeks of combined chemo-radiotherapy.

After this, I happened to pass that consultant in the corridor and he met me with eyes that held a look of pity, combined with a little awkwardness. As we passed, he acknowledged me with a small smile with sad eyes and then quickly looked away. It puzzled me for a moment, until I realised that he was looking on me as the daughter of a cancer patient. What he might not have realised, was that I've been here a couple of times before and Dad with his charm, wit and humour made us laugh more than cry. 'I'll beat this kid,' he said with a smile after the consult. I asked Mum as we were washing our hands in the ladies' room, 'Does he even get what he's about to go through?' 'He probably will sail through it with an attitude like that', Mum replied.

That night in the hotel, Mum shared the story of when she met Dad. She described difficult parts of her childhood in the Philippines that were previously closed off from me. She explained how much anger she had inside from this. 'I'm awful to you at times,' she said to him when they were dating, 'Why would you stay with me?' 'I love you. I can't help it,' he replied.

'and slowly, slowly, he broke my walls down,' she reflected, 'it's my turn to be here for him now.'

The next day, we had a visit from Nicola from radiotherapy. She had the most amazing bedside manner. She was gifted with the most fantastic rapport and ease, with appropriate humour. Her clinical skills matched her communication skills. We felt confident that Dad had a thorough assessment and work up for treatment. There was a question as to whether the prostate should be treated alongside the bowel cancer. This needed discussion with the urology and colorectal teams.

In no time, the colorectal team visited, and the consultant delegated to his residents, the task of contacting Rockhampton for the urology records. I pulled one of the residents aside after her boss left and introduced myself. I said quietly and with a smile, 'I can save you loads of time.' I produced a USB with a summary document collating 27 attachments; outlining the whole history of Dad's leukaemia and prostate cancer. She smiled back and nodded, taking me behind the nurse's station to load up the files. She asked me how much I understood of the latest. I said that I understood that the bowel tumour was cancer, which had to be removed, followed by chemo and radio, and that there was no spread. She informed that the tumour was circular in shape, which is more typical of a primary. I really appreciated the time she took to explain this to me and without even asking, she printed off all the scan and pathology reports from this episode and handed them to me. So I was grateful to have more light reading for the plane.

Alex arrived the next day, and over a couple beers he shared that when it comes to matters of human relationships, he often struggles to connect. He used to think that the problem was the way others were with him. 'But I realise now, that it's what I put out, that makes it difficult for others to reach me. My problem now, is that I don't know how to change.' My heart felt for him, because it must be such a difficult place to be. 'Having insight is a good start I guess', not knowing what else to offer. I have always craved deeper connection with Alex but felt pushed away or avoided when I got too close. I stopped short of mentioning this though, for fear of making him feel worse. 'I feel lost at times,' he continued, 'Like I'm just going through the motions in life without any direction or purpose.' I shared that I care deeply and can recognise that quality in others. 'I see it in you. All that I can do is make the most of these short visits. I feel grateful that I can support with my clinical background but wish that I had the option to make it my purpose to be there for them on a more regular basis. Of course, you don't have to take this option, but here is an opportunity to be there for Mum and Dad. Hard times are up ahead.'

Mum returned to Rockhampton for a short time and then joined Dad again in Brisbane for the remainder of his treatment. She was obviously wonderful company and the meals that she prepared for him in the accommodation became famous. The smell of her stir fries drove people crazy! She's also a deft and speedy hand at crochet, so when sitting with Dad during chemo, she made beanies for the kids under treatment. Mum said to me on the phone that they, 'all adore your Dad. We arrived early once because of the bus schedule and we were of course willing to wait, but reception insisted on bringing his slot forward, saying 'We would do anything for him.' In fact, at the end of his course of treatment his consultant said, and I can't imagine he would say this to every patient, 'It has been an honour and a privilege to serve you.' Dad proved the power of responding to any situation with a positive mindset and attitude. He not only beat it, he sailed through the treatment

....or at least that's the impression I got from the UK. Olivia happened to mention that Mum spoke of days when Dad couldn't even lift is head off the sofa. Dad's courage, strength and selfless kindness through this whole episode was unforgettable. Alex also completely stepped up to and over the plate. He moved up to Rockhampton and held the fort while they were in Brisbane and took care of everything quietly in the background when they returned home.

Chapter 7

Correspondence with Rockhampton

Dear Dad,

I'm writing this on the plane from Brisbane just reflecting on our week together and I have the biggest smile on my face. I feel grateful for all the little moments of laughter and connection that we had. I never stop learning from your example. Your courage, positivity and quiet strength are such an inspiration to me.

I was truly moved, when after speaking with Uncle Col on the phone, you commented that the waiting time on your scope was, 'only fair,' as there must have been others with higher priority. It seems to me that you live out your belief in fairness and equity to the extent that it has become part of your very nature. So it may come as a surprise to you that I find it so extraordinary that you are uncompromising with sticking to your principles, even when your health is on the line.

I wish I was there when you came out with your cleverly placed crowd pleaser, 'Welcome to my humble abode.' Your empathy and your capacity to put the needs of others ahead of your own is a quality that defines your character. Thanks to you, service above self is one of my most precious guiding principles. Through my youth though, I was out to help everyone, to the extent that I neglected my own wellbeing. I've since learned to reign it in, so that I can focus my energies on where I can have the greatest impact.

Mum's also taught me to build on myself first, to be of greater service to others. She's also helped me see the wisdom in accepting help from others as well. During this trip, Mum and I spent many a fun time. I've enjoyed seeing Mum (likely down to your influence) mellow over the years. We had long chats about her past and it's helped me admire her even more, which I thought was impossible!

I even got one night where Alex and I spent quality time, as Mum slept through. As you of course know, Alex is like his dad – of uncompromising character, loyal and kind. I believe that we'll see more of Alex come to the surface in times ahead.

It's a shame that Olivia and Seth couldn't make it, but I completely understand.

Despite being on the other side of the world, I always feel part of this amazing family. I feel so fortunate to be able to have you both as my parents. This week will stay with me forever.

I love you so much,   Julie xxooxx

Dad's comment that others must have had higher priority than him, got me thinking about size of the healthcare problem. From subsequent reading and research, I learned that Queensland is the only state in Australia, where more people live outside the capital than inside of it. At 2012, the population of Greater Brisbane was 2.19 million, accounting for nearly half of Queensland's population. The remainder of Queensland was 2.37 million, spread over 5 towns with populations ranging from approximately 100,000 to half a million. The rest were scattered in smaller towns along a huge coastline. Rockhampton was the biggest town in Central Queensland, with a population of 62,000.

I can't imagine it's an easy task sourcing so many small regional centres over such a large area. It's not just equipment that's costly, but supplying expertise is a big challenge. Top doctors, unless they've moved rural as a lifestyle choice, tend to base themselves in a city. They can be on-call to several large hospitals and work with the strongest teams and latest technology. Resources are centralised, because funding has to be proportional to the population served. This means that while rural hospitals suffer, the major city hospitals have a huge catchment, seeing the complex, weird and wonderful. As a result, they're world class. Dad having to stay in Brisbane for his latest treatment, is roughly the equivalent of those living in the northernmost part of Scotland, travelling to London for radiotherapy! Rockhampton is almost too big and too small, because they are a main referral hub for the region of Central Queensland, yet are still relatively small in population and remotely located in the broader picture.

Regardless of the reason, repeated delays in the same patient, suggested a pattern to me, which I felt duty bound to flag up. Besides, I had loads of time to write a letter on the plane. I hoped that raising these issues might even provide support for increased funding. Soon after I arrived home, I emailed my letter to Dr Coffey, then Director of Medical Services at Rockhampton. It outlined the timelines of Dad's care and raised concerns that a patient with known leukaemia waited over a year from the time of initial GP referral to receiving a biopsy result for prostate cancer. I also raised concerns that PR bleeding in that same patient, was left on a waiting list for a colonoscopy until an acute bleed presented 6 months later.

There was a delay in response because the director was out of region, so Andrea, his PA contacted us in July informing that the case was referred to the acting Medical Director, Dr Cumming. Andrea invited us to discuss the case with Dr Cumming and Dr Atherstone from surgery, with my father if he wishes to. Dad was happy for me to proceed without including him in discussions. The 5th August was confirmed, but when the agreed time (7.15am UK) was reached, Dr Cumming attended the call and informed that the time clashed with surgical handover. The 16th August at 4.30pm was pencilled in and then moved to the 22nd August. No wonder they took forever to get Dad's diagnoses!

During the meeting, their version of the timeline was read out by Dr Cumming. Dad was booked for a Category 1 outpatient consult and seen in hospital 12 days after his GP referral for the bleed. He was seen by a registrar, who discussed his case with the consultant. The categorisation wasn't likely discussed, as it was booked as a Category 2 for the colonoscopy. 'But It should have been a Cat 1,' Dr Atherstone added, 'but even as a Cat 2, it should have taken 3 months not 6 to come through.' Dr Cumming continued to explain that they flagged this case in their mortality meeting and all agree that it should have been a Cat 1, which is 'extremely unfortunate, acknowledged and regretted.' This was rattled off quickly at the end of the sentence, as though he was reading it off the written timeline. Nice…. Heartfelt. It was extremely 'unfortunate, acknowledged and regretted,' that my Dad now has a permanent stoma and a rear end wound infection, I thought.

'The junior doctors have been informed to consult the senior doctors regards the categorisation,' Dr Cumming continued, 'The doctors who made the decision have since moved onto a different secondment - but as we are led to believe, it was booked as a Cat 2, because the bleeding was presumed to be radiation prostatitis.' Wow. They hadn't exactly done their research prior to this meeting. I informed that Dad didn't have treatment to his prostate. 'I see,' replied Dr Atherstone, taking a moment to respond, 'I'm…I'm not aware of these things, I'm just trying to think on reasons why.' I asked that they locate the colleagues who made the decision to confirm the facts; which they agreed to do. I also asked if the case had been flagged through their reporting systems, which they couldn't confirm, but would get back to me on.

7th September 2013

Tears filled my eyes on hearing how Dad had to suffer such indignity, so needlessly on his transfer back to Rockhampton hospital. Brisbane held off on releasing Dad to ensure that staff on the other end were prepared and when satisfied that a bed was available, a doctor to receive his case and the wound vac would be reconnected right away; they boarded him for his flight. Despite making these communications, on arrival, the hospital was unaware of his case. He arrived at approximately 3pm on Wednesday 4th September and stayed on a temporary bed in a side room at A+E until a bed was found at 9pm.

Because the wound still wasn't connected to the vac next day, the smell from the infection was so strong that despite his hunger, Dad was unable to eat his lunch. When my Mum came to visit, she was unable to tolerate the smell and had to leave the room. Even one of the nurses commented sympathetically and whilst Mum made 3 requests to chase up progress on the arrival of the stoma nurse, the only choice was to wait, as there was only one in the hospital

The wound vac was finally reconnected at 3pm on Thursday 5th September. At this point Dad asked to have the bedding changed, as it was in a poor state. Half an hour later they asked again, as Mum took him to the shower. Whilst fresh bedding had been placed in the room in the meantime, the bed was not yet made. Mum made the bed herself so that Dad could return to bed in comfort. Due to the wound pain, he couldn't sustain much walking or sitting.

Sam was furious when I told him about it, 'This is disgusting,' he began, 'Sue them!' I guess as a healthcare practitioner, I wanted to believe that raising discussion through due process would make a change. I didn't want to take from a system that was already stretched by pursuing compensation. I helped Mum write a complaint letter raising the issue that, in addition to the unpleasantness and indignity, the potential risk of worsening Dad's wound site was increased. Given that he was MRSA positive, diabetic and immunosuppressed from chemo/radiotherapy, 24 hours off the wound vac could prove costly to Dad's recovery. We asked for an explanation as to where communication links failed.

The following week, word came back from the August telecoms with the Doctors. They had received a response from the registrar involved in booking Dad's colonoscopy. Dr Coffey who had returned to post, wrote on behalf of the registrar,

'After review of the case notes written at the time, he stated that he remembered your father and was most concerned to hear what had happened. His recall of events was that after discussion with senior staff, your father was categorised as a Category 2 urgency for a colonoscopy because the bleeding had stopped, he was not seriously affected by it, and because the waiting time for Category 2 urgency was about 6 weeks. Clearly your father did not have his appointment for colonoscopy within the expected time, and the reason for this is now being followed up.'

October 2013

Dear Juliana

Sorry for the delay in response.

Investigation into the waiting times for bookings has shown that some Category 2 bookings were achieved within 6 weeks, but not all. Therefore it is understandable that if any registrar had experienced patients returning within 6 weeks for review after booking, and been unaware of others waiting longer, they may have assumed that all patients were being seen on time.

Out-patient management staff have been made aware of the circumstances surrounding your father and are working hard at ensuring there is regular review of urgency to prevent a similar episode in future. Current medical staff are also aware and will be more rigorous with classifications if there is doubt about potential delay.

On behalf of the hospital I apologise for the delay that occurred and trust that your father will benefit from his ongoing treatment.

Do all the medical directors in that place read from the same bullshit book of apologies? Some referrals were taking longer than 6 weeks, ah…like 6 months, but how were we to know? Anyway, we've told our current team of the problem, so that'll fix it. Sorry about that and I trust that his care will be fine from here on in. I trust not!

When updating Claire on the latest, she agreed with Sam on pursuing a lawsuit. 'My dad's right on this one,' she said. 'The only way that organisations listen and take real action, sadly, is to hit them in the pocket.' Claire was moving up into management circles at the private hospital where she worked.

'They put sums aside for malpractice claims and once liability is accepted, they're more motivated to action changes to prevent future payouts.' I was starting to come around to their view. Soon after, a news story broke, detailing that Dad's urologist was under malpractice charges for taking the wrong kidney out of a patient. Bloody hell! There were also 3 more surgeries being investigated. I contacted the legal firm who acted as media commentators on the hospital. They responded far quicker than the hospital funnily enough. The paralegal asked me to supply details of the losses in income or expenses incurred as a result of the negligence.

At the time, Dad had a date coming up for a prostate operation (TURP) because he was experiencing problems with his waterworks again. Mum asked me in an exasperated tone, 'Why didn't they just treat the prostate back in Brisbane?' 'I know,' I said, 'but decisions can only be made at the time weighing up the risks and with predictions looking forward. Unfortunately, predictions aren't an accurate science.' The upshot was that with his urologist currently suspended, surgeries were being referred to the neighbouring private hospital and Dad was due for surgery next week. With Dad needing to just focus on staying positive and Mum already feeling frustrated, I decided that now was not the time to get into an adversarial mindset with the hospital.

In response to the latest press, an inquiry led by Central Queensland was called. The board inquiry Chair, Charles Ware, stated in an ABC article.

'It is obvious that we have systemic failure in patient safety systems, so we have taken action to address those – firstly by terminating the appointment of the executive director of medical services and the director of surgery.'

www.abc.net.au/news/2014-05-06/doctor-under-investigation-over-4-operations-at-rockhampton-hosp/5432892

I detailed a 5-page letter for the attention of the inquiry Chair. Confirmation came back that it was received, and I was referred to the patient Liaison officer Hayley Horan and the director of nursing Sandy Munro. At the time, Dad had his post op urology appointment, which would reveal biopsy results of the removed prostate tissue. His consultant mentioned me in that session as the daughter who was, 'making some noise.' I mentioned this to Hayley, pointing out how inappropriate this comment was.

A response landed in January 2015, apologising for delays to the diagnoses and for comments made by his consultant. 'I'll give you noise,' I thought as I looked up the details of the solicitors. The firm expressed sympathy, but informed that the cost of pursuing a claim would exceed the compensation sought. I wondered how many others she had to say this to, when I read the following story:

'The head of Maurice Blackburn Queensland medical negligence department has already had cases against the hospital, and has two other ongoing cases. But Ms Atkinson said there were many who did not have their day in court because the legal fees would not be covered by the potential compensation.'

www.themorningbulletin.com.au/news/lawyer-tells-of-horror-stories-from-patients/2250913/

Chapter 8

Cancelled trip and Mum's 60th

O ur 10th Wedding anniversary was coming up and we wanted to celebrate the occasion with friends and family in Oz. I booked flights via Hong Kong with a stopover in a luxury hotel and booked a country getaway holiday home north of Sydney, near Uncle Col's family. At the same time however, a unit for my practice became available on a on a rural estate with uninterrupted views of the countryside, just 3 miles from town.

It was a 1250 square foot sandstone barn conversion. Like moving from renting a room in a flat in your twenties, to getting your own place; it felt like the right time to grow up. It was quite a step up in overheads though, and there was a smaller unit which would have been less risky, but less suitable for gait analysis. I agonised over the pros and cons of each for a couple of weeks until Sam, fed up of my indecision came out with, 'Just grow a pair and get the bigger unit.'

Being such a beautiful building, renovated to such a high standard; I wanted to do the space justice and went for the 5-star hotel look. I kitted it out from scratch, complete with a video treadmill video gait analysis system. I can see how budgets blow out on renovation shows. Everything cost more and took longer than planned. At this point I was committed to the vision and wanted to see it through; so was having doubts as to whether a trip to Oz was the best timing. There were political protests that had surfaced in Hong Kong, and although they turned out to be relatively low key, there was no predicting how China might have reacted. If we cancelled with a few months' notice, we could be refunded the accommodation deposits and taxes on the flights, but if we committed the balance, we stood to lose a lot more. We decided to cancel, much to the disappointment of my family, but they understood.

With my focus firmly on developing the practice now, I hired and trained reception staff. A very talented Podiatrist and Sports Massage Therapist joined the team. The next thing I knew, I had my hands full with compliance, Health and Safety, websites, social media, marketing, technology, reception staff appraisals, protocols, accounts. etc. I woke up complaining one morning to Sam about how much there was to do and my frustrations over the fact that my associates and staff didn't always share my vision or understand my pressures. I went on and on like this and when he was able to find a gap in my rhetoric he simply said, 'You sound like Derek lately.' Derek was a compulsive complainer at Sam's work. This comment stopped me in my tracks. 'Do I?' I asked, shocked. 'Having the practice, team and job of your dreams, I don't know why you're not having more fun.' He was so right and with that, I proceeded to have the best time ever. We even recovered the setup costs in the first year.

Then Mum suffered a heart attack. No surprises given the stress that she was under to support Dad while he was convalescing. She was raging about some idiot that she was working with and came down with crushing chest pain. She was transferred to hospital and was in for a few days. 'I'm fine', she said with her usual tough as nails, optimistic tone, 'I don't think it was even a heart attack, just stress.' 'Mum, you stress me out!' I growled mockingly. 'Make sure you follow Drs orders, ok?' She promised. Her 60th Birthday was coming up in a couple of months and I had declined the invite as I was still settling into the clinic. 'It changes nothing,' I declared sensibly. Sam looked deeply into my eyes, waiting for the tears to come, 'You know it changes everything.' I cried in his arms.

  The week before I was due to fly, Olivia texted to check that I was still coming. To which I replied 'Of course.' She informed that she would be unable to make it because her son was teething. I was thrown because this was the second time that she wasn't meeting up. When I travelled to Brisbane, she passed up the visit and never actually visited Dad at any time when he was being treated for his cancer. Mum pointed out in her defence, that she did phone regularly, unlike Seth who disappeared. Having spoken to a friend in a similar situation, she shared that all the care of her ill mother fell onto her. Her half brothers and sisters split the scene. She explained that as my father was not Olivia and Seth's biological dad, they may not feel the same way about things as I do. This had helped up until now, but this was Olivia's Mum we were talking about, who recently had a heart attack and is inviting everyone to her 60th.

I replied that I was disappointed that she would be missing a catch up again and her reply came back with, 'My children will always come first, this is something you may never understand.' Wow. I would die for Sarah. I understand that love is love, whether I have biological children or not. I also understood that Olivia's tendency of not putting herself out for others pre-dated having her children. I made the mistake of sharing that last thought and the conversation escalated into a text war. It ended in me suggesting that she could, 'have features of narcissism and that I hope that she seeks professional help.' It was a step too far that Sam advised against sending. I knew the risk of retaliation or damage to the relationship, but at that point, I felt that I had nothing to lose. I felt that our relationship had been so one sided and so damaged for so long, that I was ready to end it unless there was a chance that she might seek help. Sam was right, the comment only served to raise her defences rather than encourage reflection.

In truth, Olivia's retort was accurate - I'm not a psychologist. Further, my map of the world has its biases coming from my own skewed perspective. I reflected that it was more important that I understood my part in this rather than anyone else's.

"Put down the magnifying glass and pick up the mirror."

I was a textbook people pleaser, a co-dependent. My personality in relationship was based on a self-sacrificial kind of love. I gave and gave and loved with all my heart; anyone who touched my life. I was the person who would drop everything, fly across the world, spend all the cash in my possession to come to the rescue. I did everything I could do to make others happy. To wrap up and nurture those I loved. I even joined a profession to help people out of pain.

Years before this conflict with my sister, I started to realise that there were problems with living this way. Loving in this way can be enabling to those who aren't behaving responsibly. Rather than helping them grow, it can keep them stuck. When I've come to the rescue, it's negated the need for others to find their own way and learn and to take responsibility. Whilst it always came from a place of love, it could be harmful and sometimes, loving from a distance, or tough love would be a kinder response.

I recognise the pattern of *rescuing* others from my earliest relationships. I would complete Alex's assignments at school and stay up all night helping Olivia with her university work to stop them getting into trouble. The bigger trouble was that they learnt that they could keep waiting until the last minute, because their sister would save the day. My well-intentioned caring could overflow into controlling, as trying to 'fix' other people's problems in this way, resulted in me feeling let down when they inevitably failed to learn the lesson.

When Dad was in ICU, being treated for the acute bowel bleed, I jumped on a plane without a second's thought for the possibility that Intensive Care in a rural hospital is like a High Dependency Unit elsewhere. This distinction was the difference between being on life support or not. The last thing I expected was for him to be sitting up eating breakfast when I arrived at Brisbane. Not that of course I wasn't relieved, but a moment's pause to assess the situation and ask myself if I needed to spring into rescue mode, may have resulted in a planned journey rather than emergency cancelling all my patients and paying top bill to rush at a moment's notice across the world. Assuming the role of the helper / carer / fixer/ rescuer, featured me nowhere in this equation. Through my own doing, I have given and given and loved and cared for everyone else but me.

In always coming last, time runs out for me and I neglect my own health, peace, personal space and well-being.

Another problem with this tendency, is that I've found myself disappointed when others haven't put themselves out for family in the same way that I would. However, it's possible that these individuals have a more balanced sense of self and so don't feel the need to jump to the rescue in a self-sacrificial kind of way. I've often called people out for being self-centred, selfish or even narcissistic for making different choices to me. Not very loving of me, despite viewing myself the caring and compassionate type for acting in this way. Instead of judging and persecuting Olivia, maybe I could learn from her more developed sense of self. I needed to learn that It's not selfish to take care of myself.

Mum was in hospitality and catering and had managed businesses (including her own) throughout her career, so organising a 60th birthday party was no trouble at all. I was always amazed at how effortless she made entertaining look. 'Is there anything I can help with,' I asked when I'd come around from my jetlag. As expected, she replied, 'No it's all in hand,' and she wasn't kidding!

Alex had moved to a new place a couple of suburbs down and he had a neat outdoor entertainment area, part shaded under the stilts of his Queenslander style house, so the party was at his place. The folks had put their house on the market and wanted to keep it tidy for viewings. So somehow, Mum worked her stealth in their kitchen like a ninja, without a trace of mess and transported it to Alex's place all while entertaining and feeding us in the days leading up to the BBQ style party. I couldn't even advise her to be resting, as I didn't even see her doing all this. Besides, this was resting for her: a party for only 50 people and a week off work? Piece of cake!

The house was on the market because Mum and Dad needed to downsize and wanted to travel Australia grey nomad style. Given their recent health problems, I agreed that life was too short and they should go for it. Over a coffee, Mum also happened to mention that Dad had some bleeding from his stoma tube and so returned to his consultant. At first, they booked him as a category 3 for the endoscopy but Mum questioned it and they reviewed his case. The consultant noticed that a surveillance scope was supposed to have occurred 12 months post op but it was now closer to 2 years!

The consultant rushed it through. 'Anyways,' Mum said, 'his scope was clear and he's on 5 yearly reviews.' As good as that news was, it hadn't restored my faith that Rockhampton Hospital had changed their ways.

When we arrived at Alex's house, I raised the issue with Dad. 'I think we should just let it go,' he said, 'after all there was no harm done.' 'Not for you and only by good luck and not good management - again,' I responded. 'If they can miss the mark so many times with you and this after an inquiry, what else are they missing?' Dad just wanted to leave it and I had to respect his wishes, so we got on with the business of having a party. A fabulous party it was too.

At the party though, the conversation turned to the hospital as a couple of cousins had some horror stories to report. Not a single person in our circle failed to have something happen to them or someone close to them; that amounted to negligence at best. When I woke up next morning, I couldn't shake that conversation from my head and the sense of needing to do something about it. Over breakfast I said, 'Dad, you taught me to stand up for what is right and fair and to speak up when you should for others. I feel that this is one of those times.' Dad nodded and let Mum and I get on with it. Within 48 hours, we had a meeting with Hayley (the patient liaison) to cover outstanding queries. We formed some questions to ask the Director of Nursing (Sandy), who wasn't available to attend.

After that meeting, we had an appointment with one of the big commercial television stations. The minute that I mentioned that my Dad's urologist was the 'wrong kidney guy,' they offered a timeslot right away. It was an odd experience. They sat us down in a studio and the line of questioning was clearly directed towards capturing a headline. The wider issues didn't seem important. Within minutes, they asked the questions that had my mum in tears and me comforting her. Bingo, this would make great television. That was a take.

I felt a little uncomfortable that they would report in such a sensationalised way and I wanted to give the hospital a chance to respond to our latest meeting. One of my friends said that once the media have hold, you'll have lost all control and the hospital will stop communicating with you, so I held off on running the story. On reflection, I should have just let them run with it.

Chapter 9

Dissertation and other dramas

I hired my school friend Lindsay as a coach whilst managing my team. She was an excellent personality profiler and her assessments helped me understand the team dynamic. This time I was after some coaching to get my head in the game for my dissertation. I had deferred the last year of university to get my team settled into the new unit, but that year had flown by.

As always, it was a great session and I was able to get hold of my motivation. This work would reflect all learning that has gone before regards evidence-based practice and what it really means to me as a clinician. With more experience and a bigger picture view since my last dissertation, I was in touch with the importance of forming appraisal skills and my own position. 'Nice work,' affirmed Lindsay. For you to stay focussed, this work has to mean something to you.

I also needed to clear time for this commitment. I had already begun to question my continued involvement with the movement screening company. I was working and travelling for meetings as if I led a corporate life, but without the corporate income. Or any income for that matter. The promises of paid work seemed elusive even to those who completed their tutor exams; which I had yet been offered the opportunity to sit. These would involve more travel, study time and a fee.

I was also becoming increasingly disillusioned with the limitations of the product and the role itself. There was some manipulation by Saskia at play. On my visits down to head office, I would stop over at her home. This seemed a convenient way to catch up and a gesture to save me costs. It also meant that she had access to me day and night to get as much work out of me as possible. At times, I felt more like a personal assistant than a student. From running errands, to walking her dog, the boundaries between work and friendship blurred. As she became more familiar, poor behaviour increased. There were only so many times that I could accept apologies from Bruce. Each time he flew in from Europe for his teaching, he seemed to allocate time to the inevitable task of smoothing out team conflicts, largely created by Saskia.

I decided to cut my losses and notch it up to experience. I had the intention of leaving on good terms, citing competing study commitments. What I hadn't expected was a £3000 bill for their training of me! According to the contract, I owed them for their time investment, as I had not completed the programme. This was a charge of £150 per day for the privilege of setting the room, refreshments, sourcing participants through my own contacts, marketing and supporting the tutors on the courses. Attendance had been arranged in my own time. My travel and accommodation expenses, borne by me, had run into the thousands already.

I sought the advice of a solicitor and he informed that I should never have signed the contract. To dispute an agreement, I would have to demonstrate that they failed in their obligations and since it was such a one-sided contract, they had no obligations.

As the saying goes,

'Education is when you read the fine print.

Experience is what you get if you don't.'

On advice, I suggested that we come to an arrangement because of the work I contributed. As a gesture of goodwill, they offered to halve the bill and allow payment in instalments. The other option was for me to continue to market their product for a further 18 months. As I had an integrity issue with promoting something that I no longer believed in, I took the first option. Sam was up for taking the issue to small claims court, but I was feeling harassed by the whole affair and just wanted to end any contact with the company to move on.

I caught up with my old Adelaide buddy Tessa, soon after this unpleasant situation. She was working with an international circus company and was sent to attend a conference in Scotland. After the first day of lectures, we caught up on life over a Jamie Oliver pasta meal. We laughed about the time that Nathan tweaked his hamstring to impress her in an epic high kick outside the exam room. Sadly, Nathan and Tessa's marriage ended a couple of years ago. She shared with me the story of the breakup over a glass of vino to wash down our dessert and I was so impressed with the maturity and forgiveness that she expressed. Knowing Tessa, it must have been a hard time – she's so pure in love and wears her heart on her sleeve.

Matters moved onto the more recent business of finding the cute Danish guy that she met the day before at the conference. She never got to give him her number and there was only one day to go! We toasted to a promise to search for him tomorrow. In the exhibitor's hall, we went in search of her Danish pastry during morning tea. I spotted a stand manned by Saskia and her company. Out of their line of sight and earshot, I shared the history with Tessa. She nodded in understanding and shared a story of a company that threatened to ensure that she never worked for anyone in physio teaching if she left. Not to be daunted by bullies, she left as planned. Then, either unperturbed in her mission to find her guy, or to help me to face my fears, or maybe both, she dragged me right past Saskia's stand! It was a shame that things ended the way that they did. I would have liked to stay on friendly terms. Yet there I was, not even wanting to say hi to this colleague.

I had another visitor landing soon. My gorgeous niece Paige, was on a Futsal (indoor football) tournament that was touring the UK. I was getting frustrated with trying to get an itinerary from Seth, who was doing his usual uncontactable thing. Mum couldn't get the information for me either, but as soon as Paige suffered dehydration on landing into the UK, I was contacted right away. I spoke with her coach, and she was recovering just fine. I was a little annoyed that it took this situation to get her details, but I was pleased that I could at least plan to watch her play.

Now in her early teens, I was worried that Paige wouldn't remember me. The last time we caught up, she was a little page girl at Olivia's wedding. Though the moment I entered the pitch side, she ran towards me to for the hugest hug. Sam made a teasing remark that she wasn't, 'a real footballer, because you don't spit.' Without missing a beat, Paige smiled ironically and said, 'It's indoor.' 'That's my girl,' I laughed as I gave her a high five. Sam was unusually speechless. She was growing up to become a wonderful young lady, quietly confident in her own skin; reaching this stage far earlier in life than her Auntie Jules did. I joined the team out shopping in Newcastle, and I bought her a pair of sparkly football boots. She shyly insisted that she didn't want anything, but I really wanted something for her to take home and remember our catch up, whenever she played.

Things may be distant with my brother Seth, but I wasn't letting that affect my precious connection with his lovely daughter.

The next week, I received a text from Seth. 'Paige has sore knees, could you check in on her – she might just need some of that magic spray or something.' I was incensed and pointed out that he only got in touch when he needed something and that it was not okay to use me in this way. Besides, I thought, the last thing that I wanted to do professionally was to travel to the other side of the country and show up to a junior team, (that had no physio cover) and offer my assessment. He replied that, 'This is not about us, but about your niece.' 'How dare you put that on me when the only reason that I could even catch up with Paige here, was because you wanted me to rush to her rescue when she landed.' I ran this text by Sam before sending, to avoid the risk of overreacting and alienating another family member. Sam agreed that it's important to set boundaries. 'Let's just leave it for now,' came back Seth's reply. I checked in with Paige directly and her knees weren't an urgent matter.

I had a meeting lined up with a potential supervisor for my dissertation. She put her name as a contact on one of the research projects running at the university. The meeting went well, and I was invited to meet the research team the following week. In my usual capacity to pull crazy hours to meet a deadline, I sourced all the reviews on the topic that I could locate and extracted the data onto a massive colour coded spreadsheet over the weekend. 'You'll run this meeting,' Sam remarked. 'No way,' I replied, 'I'm the boss in my clinic. I'm just a lowly student here.'

This was echoed by the chief investigator of the project who commented, 'So you're the master's student. You're here to sit, watch and be quiet.' Nice. At least I know my place I thought. As the meeting proceeded, it appeared that no one had done much background prep for the meeting. In fact, only one person in the team of six – my supervisor, had a blank pad of paper and pen. When they started speculating over information that I had already scoped, I asked if I might comment. Before I knew it, I had opened the spreadsheet and the whole team was listening in earnest. The chief investigator clocked the death stare that I was receiving from my supervisor and she turned the laptop away, changing the subject. Sam laughed when I told him, 'I knew you'd end up running the meeting.'

The next day I received an email from the dissertation module leader informing that my project can't be the same as the team's but can be related to it. Strange, I thought. They were the ones that published the question on their call for students. No matter, I decided to perform a review of the review papers on the topic. A study more focussed on the methodology of the reviews, could perhaps lead into their review of the primary research.

My supervisor was on board with a tertiary review, but problems started when I drafted the proposal. Numerous red penned edits came back and she commented that my scientific writing style was a problem. I asked a friend who lectured in medicine to have an honest look at my writing as I was prepared to take a course to rectify the problem if needed. 'You write beautifully,' came back his response. He explained that my supervisor was treating me more like a post doc, probably to impress. He suggested that I ask the module leader for a new supervisor. A little daunted by this idea, I worked up the courage to have the conversation. The module leader was surprisingly receptive. 'You wouldn't be at this stage of the programme if you couldn't write at level 7,' she commented.

We agreed that I would first discuss my concerns with my supervisor without mentioning that I'd spoken with the module lead prior.

The discussion didn't go well. We agreed to disagree and send an email to the module lead. On verifying her summary of my view, I asked her to correct a point, to which she snapped back, 'No. It might be *your* dissertation, but this is *my* email and it's going in as is.' I was stunned, almost to the point of laughing. She started to shout, and I thought to myself, that if I wasn't entitled to disagree without her shouting over me, I was making the right decision. I calmly informed her that this meeting was over and walked out.

I learned afterwards, that I was her first MSc student and that I would be allocated to the person that was supervising her (the chief investigator no less). A little awkward; not only for undermining her, but also because I happened to hear that this new supervisor, wasn't after an MSc student this year. If that was true, she didn't let on. Though perhaps because I was carrying the 'troublemaker student' label already, she took no time in controlling our first meeting with outlining the 'rules of engagement' before I was able to say much at all. To be fair, I preferred this approach as I knew where I stood, and her experience definitely showed. I received more from that phone call than several hours with her subordinate.

Fast forward to November 2016 and I was grappling with differences with my new supervisor on how to proceed. Her suggestion was to just toe the line and treat it like a tick box exercise. 'I'm not being funny, but it's just an MSc, not Nobel Prize winning research.' she remarked. I figured that I wasn't in the running for a Nobel prize, but my issue was that the work wouldn't even be valid as a piece of research if I go with her suggestion. I tried to object again, and she shouted loudly, 'NO!' as if I was a 3-year-old. 'I'm 39 tomorrow,' I said to Sam afterwards, 'What the hell?'

Having taken Lindsay's coaching advice and invested meaning into my purpose, I just couldn't go with my supervisor's suggestion. Perhaps I invested too much meaning to the point of obsession at times, but this wasn't my first thesis and I was in no rush to do another anytime soon. After all I learned in Adelaide and Keele, how could I just fail to show up? I was distracted from this thought when the phone rang.

'Alex has seen the doctor as he's had trouble passing water,' Mum began on the phone. The GP ordered some tests and has referred to an urologist. After waiting a few weeks, Mum checked that the referral had been received from specialist outpatients and learned that the ball had been dropped. The GP re-sent it and it was now with them. I was absolutely furious. These guys are consistent at least… As I still hadn't heard back from the last set of concerns regards Dad last year, I decided to prepare an email to chase this and raise this latest issue. Alex might even see the 'wrong kidney guy.' I learned from reading online, that his position had been reinstated! I also learned that there were investigations under way due to the death of a baby and injuries to 3 others in Rockhampton Hospital the last 12 months. Over this, the head of central QLD health resigned, and others happened to transfer interstate. I looked up the current hospital board and printed off their mug shots to pin on my wall.

Dear Hayley,

This email is following the meeting that we had on Monday 17th August 2015. We have still been waiting for answers to questions that we raised. Unsatisfied with the lack of communication, we have sought advice and have made our own investigations. Through obtaining the latest medical records, we have been able to clarify several points regarding my father's case and the timeline around the episode under discussion.

In addition to these questions, a new and more urgent issue has arisen which requires your attention….

….Having experienced unreasonable delays in my father's case, our family is understandably concerned and distressed by the latest delay in my brother's. In Alex's case there are 3 specific issues that I urge your team to consider when deciding on priority for early diagnosis.

1. That one month has already passed from the time of Alex's GP contact.

2. That the family history of cancer needs to be highlighted in decision making.

3. The age of my brother puts him at increased risk of aggressive prostate cancer (research evidence attached).

My family are anxiously awaiting confirmation of the categorisation of the urology consultation in advance of an appointment for Alex. Whilst we can't change what has happened in the past as regards my father, I sincerely hope that nothing similar would occur with regards my younger brother.

I managed to speak with Alex the next day and learned more history and test results. Perhaps to keep a lid on it, I was too procedural in asking questions. He responded in a defensive fashion, erupting with accusations to stop making a fuss and, 'just leave it alone. It's my life and has nothing to do with you!' I blew back up at him by saying, 'Don't you dare make this all about you! The whole family is concerned and there are bigger issues. Here is a hospital that has a consistent pattern of failing it's community.' He later texted to apologise. I had already let it go, as I understood how emotionally charged this situation was.

When reading up on the evidence for interpreting his results, I found myself in floods of tears. His ultrasound revealed that the prostate was enlarged and there was void residue. His prostate bloods were within the under 50 age range supplied by pathology, but according to a systematic review it was above recommended values for the 31-40-year-old range. His white cell count was up too. All the times that I had to face news regarding my parents, paled in comparison to how I felt in that moment. The thought of this being prostate cancer in any 36-year-old would be far more devastating, let alone it happening to my baby brother.

I emailed Hayley again and urged that an appointment be sourced as a matter of urgency. The following day, I received a reply to the first email from a Julie-Ann, the hospital's Quality, Safety & Risk Business Unit Partner, stating that it may be possible that I had not received the letter responding to my concerns regards Dad. A copy was attached.

There it was: a point by point response with an official apology on Queensland Government letterhead. Not that this meant much to me in the current circumstances. What meant more was that Alex's appointment had come through for a fortnight's time. I wasn't even surprised when that day arrived, and his urologist dismissed him as, 'too young to have prostate cancer,' and requested a cystoscopy. I had already sourced a private consult with a urologist that visits from Brisbane for a second opinion, in case something like this occurred.

Even though my brother apologised for accusing me of interfering in his life, there was some truth to what he said. Whilst it's easy to see caring as a good thing, it steps into my 'old friend' caretaking, when there's investment in controlling the outcome. In this situation with my brother, I felt that it would have been unreasonable to stay away from the situation altogether. However, I imagine his upset came from a place of not feeling in control or owning his problem. On reflection, my approach could have been more collaborative.

I came to reflect on my part much later on, because in the thick of this shit storm, the following request landed from Sarah via Facebook messenger, 'Hi there, would you mind contributing to this mother's and daughter's piece and this survey about creativity? Xx' Sarah was also in the dissertation year of her degree, in graphic design. The piece about mothers and daughters, was a tribute to mums, beginning with her story. 'My mum is the best human in my life.'

Over recent years, we were seeing less and less of **Sarah**. I guess it's typical of 22-year olds to only call when they need something, but I took it personally. Her mum lived 30 mins away from us and I had seen countless Facebook posts of her visiting from Uni and spending the weekend at her mum's without even letting us know that she was in town. I could have reasoned that this was because she had a stack of school friends to catch up with, but in that moment, reason escaped me and whilst still reactive and hurting, I replied, 'Sarah on this occasion, I won't be able to contribute to your piece. I have a lot on and am prioritising my time and efforts on people who I have a mutual relationship with.'

Sarah replied, that she didn't understand why I had to respond like that and that it had created animosity between us. Instead of stopping there, I went on to explain what brought me to this place. Looking at it now, I can't recognise the person who ever thought what I emailed was a good idea. Steven Covey advises to seek first to understand and then to be understood [2]. From a place of pain, my tendency ran precisely in the opposite direction. I felt justified at the time, but now I cringe as I read how I laid all the blame at her feet and portrayed myself as a victim who was used and taken for granted. It read to Sarah as cataloguing all her flaws and me being bitter. She cut all contact with me. 'I will never again let anyone make me feel as small and disappointing as you have made me feel,' she wrote.

'Please consider what Jules is going through at the moment. She may soon discover that her brother has a serious cancer,' Sam began to explain. 'Alex is getting little help in Australia, and there may be a number of things to consider and decide.' 'What's that got to do with me?' Sarah snapped back. 'What?!', Sam asked incredulously, 'You didn't just say that?' Sarah was adamant, 'What does *all of that* have to do with *the way* that *she* spoke to *me*?' 'Where's your empathy and compassion?' Sam was disgusted. I encouraged him to not make too much of it, 'She's just angry,' I urged. It was clear that all of this was too raw to talk down and I was devastated that I had contributed to this escalating so far.

Things fell into perspective when around the same time, **Claire** had a serious health scare. She recently had hip pain, so her colleague arranged a scan, which found a mass on her ovary. In addition, she was feeling extremely fatigued, unwell and had lost loads of weight. Further tests revealed another mass on her hyperparathyroid. Being medical, we kept a practical head on things and initially **Claire** discussed with me, whether in the worst-case scenario, insurance would cover living expenses if Mark had to support their 3 children on his own. Their youngest, Jack was 3 years old at the time. It was a gorgeous sunny day and her little ones were circling us on their bikes, as she said to me quietly, 'The worst part of it all, is that I'll miss out on seeing them grow up.' I just held her tiny frame in my arms and told her that Sam and I would be there for them. Sam wasn't going there in his head. 'The diagnosis hasn't been confirmed,' he urged. 'But it doesn't look good,' I sighed. **Sarah** hadn't seen **Claire**, Mark and the kids in years, and although I wondered whether as a half-sister, she should be told, I decided to leave that up to **Claire**.

Sam the eternal optimist, was right in refraining from jumping to conclusions. **Claire** had a condition called Multiple Endocrine Neoplasia. As the name suggests, the condition generates benign tumours throughout the body. 'Typical for something abbreviated 'MEN' to cause so much havoc,' **Claire** laughed. I reflected on how jumping to conclusions had created so much unnecessary suffering for myself. I wasn't the only clinician doing this. **Claire** was in there too and when I shared the story with a GP colleague, she was straight in with, 'Who's her consultant?' The saying, 'Clinicians, make the worst patients,' is true. I think it's because, in every class at university, there was an idiot, and no one wants their relative to be treated by the class muppet. The flip side is that there's usually just one and, on the whole, we're a professional bunch. Like my surgeon friend said when I was sharing Alex's story, 'Jules, you gotta trust the man on the ground.' Turns out he was right. The scan ordered from the second opinion; cleared any suspicion of cancer and Alex is on annual blood checks.

I was chatting with Tessa via Skype during one of the many sleep disturbed nights of late. She was in Canada at the time with Circus HQ but was considering her next move. After a very successful 10-year career, I wasn't expecting a message from out of the blue saying:

'I've left the circus'

'Really?'

'It's all good though'

'Ok...'

'I'm flying through Heathrow Christmas Eve....'

Inside of 12 minutes, I had a flight booked to meet her for lunch. 'It's not every day a friend leaves the circus,' I explained to Sam, 'besides, I could do with an adventure right now.'

Tessa shared the most amazing story about her decision to depart the circus. She stood up for herself and left on her terms. It made me think on how just over a decade ago, we were just kids doing our post grad thing in Adelaide. She was off to Barcelona next, to study healthcare innovation. On telling her about my supervisor, she simply asked, 'What's with the hostility?' I was surprised. I didn't even detect I was expressing hostility. Perhaps it had become the norm, echoing something that Sam said recently, 'You're so angry when things don't go your way right now.'

I took a good look at things and saw conflicts all over the place. Saskia, my supervisors, Rockhampton Hospital, Olivia, Seth, Alex, Sarah. It was as if the more conflict I created, the more I found. I resolved to stop colouring my view in this way and remove the hostility, animosity, anger, hurt, resentment and bitterness from my life.

"Change what you see and what you see changes."

When taking a step back, I could see that my supervisor had a point. My thesis may not win a Nobel prize or set the research world on fire, but I could do something for myself in taking the stand I choose. I was a touch sneaky in writing the piece that I wanted, under the radar of my supervisor. She only worked out what I was up to a month before it was due. Thankfully, she thought by that time, that it was good work. I passed with flying colours and, more importantly for me - with integrity intact.

To celebrate finishing my thesis, I booked a trip to Barcelona and thanked Tessa for her insight in Heathrow. It set off an entire chain of events that allowed me to see life in a much more peaceful light. When I explained the findings of my research over some tapas, I watched her reaction and realised that I had uncovered something that needed to be shared with the profession. It would require conducting the full study rather than the pilot, but I promised myself that one day I would pick that thesis up off the shelf and publish the message.

On return from Barcelona I had a Skype chat with Lindsay. She helped me see the situation with Rockhampton Hospital differently. Lindsay could see that the issue was taking a real toll, and so shared the following insight, 'Just because you *can* do something, doesn't mean that you *should*.' She was right. If there's been an injustice, it doesn't mean that I *have to* address it. Rather than launching a campaign, an all-consuming quest to point out wrong doings, sometimes it's enough to know better and model that. These are big systems and are often resistant to change,' she affirmed.

As the Zen proverb says,

> "Don't seek the truth.
>
> Just cease to cherish opinions."

Reflecting on my conflict with Sarah from this new Zen perspective, I could see that I failed to learn the lessons from falling out with Olivia. When I had needs of others, that they weren't willing or able to meet, I launched into accusing them of being selfish. Irrespective of my contribution to the relationship, my needs are just that. They're my responsibility to fulfil. I can choose to look elsewhere for my needs to be met and be more discerning regards meeting the needs of others. With respect to Sarah, I had a yearning for connection when I felt so far away from Australian friends and family all those years ago. I assumed that just because I held up a vision for our relationship, she would feel the same way. This fails to consider what Sarah may have being going through from her own perspective.

After owning my needs and letting go of expecting **Sarah** to fulfil them, I apologised for my part and proposed that we reconnect for her dad's sake; who was caught in the middle. At a minimum, we could connect from a place of mutual respect. Once I was able to see my part, I spent much time in guilt and deep remorse. I accepted that I may never hear from Sarah again and although it still hurt like hell, I was at peace with it. In the absence of response from Sarah and all attempts to reconcile exhausted, there was just one thing left to do. Forgive myself.

I'm only human and accept that good people can make poor judgements at times. If I was to look at all my decisions in relationship with Sarah, the good easily outweigh the bad. Even though there are 2 parties involved, I accepted that there may be long term consequences from my recent poor judgement. That's up to Sarah. What I can do is let the wounds of self-accusation heal and forgive myself, move on and take lessons from the experience.

As the Sufi saying goes:

"Let your words pass three gates:

Is it true?

Is it necessary?

Is it kind?"

Chapter 10
Broken memories

The practice seemed quiet after my masters was completed. Any time would feel quiet after submitting that piece of work of course, but my patient numbers were definitely down on last year. This was the first time I had seen this trend in all my years in private practice. Was this a result of me investing less time and energy into the practice whilst writing my thesis? Or was this part of a wider trend? Having spoken to colleagues and businesses in the area, some admitted that things were quiet for them too. Spending up on my studies and more admin support, had landed in time with a rent increase, so bills needed paying. I decided to take on some locum work, whilst I formed a plan.

In that role, I got chatting with one of my patients about my plan and ambitions for the practice. I told him that for me, it has always been about quality care over volume of work. With more skills in movement and running, the dream would be to specialise in this and work with fewer clients. I would provide to those who are after a higher end service and interested in improving their performance over a simple patch up. This very insightful patient replied, 'I just can't see how you're going to do this without taking on volume.... without that income, you'll always have a gap between where you are and where you want to be.'

I guess it did seem absurd to be talking about delivering a high-end service, when I was there as a locum to make ends meet that quarter. He was right in that I was always spending to upgrade the service, with a vision, that at some future time, I would make that transition. He added that I would have to make a choice at some point between being a physio or running the business as I lacked the budget to hire a manager. He had seen this before, giving an example of a friend who opened a childcare centre and made a very successful business of it, but only after leaving her profession to run the business. I replied with the answer that I had always given, 'I'll just work harder,' knowing even as I said the old mantra, that it sounded unconvincing. Over the past few years, few people I knew worked harder than me. Perhaps it was my flat refusal to compromise that landed me there, having that conversation.

He kindly and gently replied, 'My fear for you is that you'll run out of time.' This reality landed near to my 40th birthday. Not that I consider this old, but it was symbolic of being at a crossroads for me. Whilst I was fine with the years of work that I put into the practice; I expected that I might feel differently doing the same for another 10-15years. I had to admit that part of signing up for the locum work was a reluctance to put energy back into the practice. He made a very clear analysis of something that I had already known deep down.

The marketplace (especially with respect to insurance) has changed so much in the last decade and I had predicted for some time that the industry is likely to go down the corporate model. All it would take is Quality Care Commission compliance inspections to hit physio and I see many sole practitioners closing for lack of viability. Of course, I've changed in the last decade too. The 'big practice' no longer had any appeal, especially if it wasn't likely to support a means to 'do something cool' or 'take a stand for quality.' I had a taste of just how much time and effort it would take to build and he was right in that at least for a time, I'd have to step back from clinical practice to get that growth (and of course there were no guarantees).

When I started out, it was easy to do the work myself. When I grew into the larger space with staff, I had bigger bills to pay; forming the necessity to grow more. One of my other patients, a very successful businessman said, 'The problem with your setup is that you are the business.' If growing this business to chase after the dream, means hiring clinical staff and moving me further away from clinical practice, then I may run the risk of defeating the object. I've never been motivated by money, so the choice between running the business and being a physio was really simple. The experience of being a locum reminded me just how much I love clinical practice.

Working with personnel, proved an entirely different game to my old role, working with recruits and I was enjoying being part of something bigger than me. There were no management decisions to make apart from managing my own time and the treatment plan of the patients. I knew right away what my choice would be. Thankfully this patient was the last of my day, because I was able to hold it together enough to complete the session and shed a tear at my desk after closing the door, for the realisation of a broken dream.

September 2017

A text landed from Mum,

'Jules, Erin is really ill in hospital.'

'What, Olivia's Erin?'

'Yes, it's not looking good. He may not make it through the night.'

Poor Olivia. We hadn't been in contact since we fell out over catching up last time. Something like this has a way of putting small things behind. I had to at least let her know that I was thinking of her. I phoned the house but there was no answer. They're likely in the hospital, I thought. Normally, I wouldn't text, but I figured that it might just give her enough space to respond, if or when she wants, in her own time. The important thing was that I made the first move.

'Olivia, Mum told me that Erin is in hospital. I'm so sorry honey xx'

'Hi Jules, that means a lot. Erin got slammed with a superbug on Monday and was in ICU by Wednesday with sepsis. The family was gathered round last night as he wasn't expected to pull through. I'm getting help with prepatory grief for the boys and am writing a journal on our daily goings on for Erin. I'm taking each day at a time and just lying low for the minute xx'

I took her meaning from that text and was glad now that I had contacted with a message. She had good support around her and didn't need any additional stress. I sent a thinking of you card to the family and later, as Erin defied all odds, a get-well card to him. He had a stroke and kidney failure, but was able to recover with dialysis, speech therapy and physio. I received all updates through my folks, which I didn't mind. Olivia and I are very different people living our lives on opposite sides of the world, but she knows that I love her.

On holidays in Lanzarote, Sam and I talked over the idea of ending the lease on the clinic's unit. It would end in September 2018. To mark the occasion, we booked a trip back to this fabulous island. We imagined what it would feel like a year from now; free from the responsibilities of staff, associates, rental, rates and utilities. I didn't know what was next, but it was enough to know the next step was this necessary ending. Sam reminded me to view the whole experience as a success. I had created the practice of my dreams and it stretched my skills further and in so many more directions, than I could ever have imagined. Had it been the path that I wanted to pursue moving forward, I would have committed with all my energy and had scaled up the operation, but I knew it would be heading in the opposite direction than I intended, so it was time to place my energy into something else.

On returning from our trip, Sam casually asked me to count the number of messages that I dealt with whilst away. I counted 33. In 10 days, I reasoned that wasn't too bad. There were many more that I was able to pass onto reception to action. I had been disciplined in checking my emails only once a day whilst Sam was catching up on the morning news and once I had cleared my inbox, we enjoyed the holiday together for the rest for the day. Then I considered it another way. It's 33 too many on holidays. Taking on study alongside building up the practices and working with Saskia, was an invitation to allow my workload to cross into our personal time. When at home, there was no longer any protected downtime apart from sleep – and even then, I had been known to wake up in the middle of the night and write down work or study solutions, to get back to sleep. No major stretch then to have admin creep into 'just a little bit each day' of our holidays.

It wasn't the time that it took to deal with these messages that was the issue, it was the interruption to the flow of quality time. The 'getting away from it all' for 'downtime' concept was seriously flawed from the outset with the, 'I'll just spend 1-2 hours each morning to clear my virtual desk,' strategy. Especially since, with better planning and delegation, all queries could have been dealt with by someone else. Especially crazy, when I had already made the decision to downsize the practice anyway. It had become such a habit that crept into my life, that at first thought, I was actually ok with it. It was only on further reflection that I considered it '33 too many.'

I shared my thoughts with Sam on the flight home, as he was clever enough to plant the question that led me to this reflection in the first place. He proposed a deal. 'You arrange to be noncontactable over Christmas, and we'll book another trip away.' What better mission to mobilise my resources and focus for the last quarter of the year, than 'operation digital detox?' I shared my last holiday experience with my team and we made plans that for 10 days over Christmas, not a single query would land with me. My work mobile would stay switched off and my personal phone on flight mode (so that I could still take pics of the beach).

For the first couple of days, I did feel a little lost. I found myself looking on my phone to check social media, emails, texts, or WhatsApp, far more frequently than I'd like to admit. After that phase, I hardly remembered where I left my phone and the change to my sense of peace was palpable. I found my thoughts more present with the holiday and I had truly left work behind. Of course, I messaged friends and family a happy Christmas, but I did it from Sam's phone so that I wouldn't be tempted to check any messages on mine.

It worked a treat. I was floating back home the day after Boxing Day, refreshed and energised. That was until I awoke next day to this message from my cousin on Facebook messenger, 'Hey Jules, have you seen Mum's message? Can you call us on messenger when you can? Not urgent, but important x.' - The kind of message from family, that someone living on the other side of the world dreads. I checked my phone messages on all apps and broke my promise to myself to stay off Facebook.

There was nothing from Mum on any of these platforms so I messaged back, 'Just looked now but couldn't see anything x' Immediately the reply landed from Karen, 'Hey Cuz, Mum would like to talk to you. Can we call you on here now? X.' 'Of course x,' I replied, my heart beating faster. After the usual tech failures that accompanied several skipped heartbeats, we managed to connect.

Mum looked pretty strung out, 'It's your dad,' she started, 'I think he's losing it.' 'What? Alzheimer's?' 'No,' she replied. 'The more severe one, dementia.' This was no time to correct her. She then proceeded to rattle off all the reasons why she eventually confirmed her suspicions. When they were at my Auntie's house recently, he was unable to find his way around even though they had visited many times before. Accidents with his stoma date back about 3 months. He would go upstairs to wash and then return having forgotten to. He lowered the legs on the caravan and then asked Mum to park it, breaking 2 legs off the van and he forgot that he left the gas cooker on. My cousin continued with more evidence, 'He's nowhere near as steady on his feet as when we last caught up with him. He still recognises us and laughs in the right places but is more withdrawn. Depression is one of the symptoms....' Her voice trailed off in my mind as a screaming in my head wanted to shout, 'STOP STOP STOP!' Tears were pouring down my face, at the first I had heard of this awful account.

This all came to a head because Mum broke her right collarbone when rushing around after Dad. She tripped over the tow bar and reached out to catch her fall. She told her husband that he would have to drive to hospital. 'That's when I knew that there was a serious problem,' she recalled. 'His driving was ok in that he operated the car fine.' He stopped at the sign, but then went to pull out in the path of another driver. When screaming out for him to stop he said, 'It's OK, I'm just showing this guy who's boss.'

Normally, I'd make a dark joke out of the last story when repeating it to Sam, but I'd lost my sense of humour. After ending the call, Sam held me in his arms as I cried, gut wrenching tears of profound grief. At the thought of such a brilliant man fading into oblivion. Tears of sadness for Mum who will help him through more and more self-care, knowing that if his physical health stands up long enough, his mental faculties will decline to the point where she is no longer recognisable to him.

I went out for a coffee break with Sam, just to get a bite and sort out my thoughts. Whilst getting ready to go out, I found a crazy flight schedule that would depart tomorrow, get me to Oz to touch down for one day and then fly back in time to return to my responsibilities here. The next locum position was split into 2 roles, done especially to accommodate my preferred hours. It would have been far easier for them to just tender it out as one role, so I just couldn't mess them about for what felt like an acute situation but was actually a chronic condition. I also had my eye on a permanent role there because it was on our doorstep and in a department working with personnel. It's true that a cuppa fixes many dilemmas. By the end of that coffee and toastie, I was settled in my clarity that the best thing to do right now was to mark time, take a breath and consider the wisest action. Think on the best way that I could be of service.

One thing that my cousin said rang in my mind. Karen was looking at a short-term solution of residential care as she and Gary were due to be away on holidays in a couple of days. Mum had a frozen shoulder on the left and a fractured collar bone on her right. There was no way she could look after Dad and herself alone in Karen's house. From there, she said, *'you can work out a family plan.'* She was absolutely right. Karen had taken the first steps in an emergency but Mum has 4 children who can take it from there. So, it's not all up to me either. There would be new accommodation to arrange and a care plan. I will forever be grateful for Karen's swift, decisive action and the clarity of that statement. It moved me from a place of despair, to having the clear goal of uniting my siblings in the common purpose of looking after the folks. A commonality that could see past the differences between us - that we all care about our folks. In touch with this and through a delicate dance of communicating with each one, I was able to express that I have commitments here. Whilst I can't be there right now, I will do what I can from the UK. Everyone was able to get their issues out of the way and be in alignment with the shared goal.

By 2am (UK time), family politics had been successfully negotiated and we were all on one Facebook conversation thread. A definite improvement from numerous disjointed conversations. In this time Dad had also seen the GP, had a blood test, cognitive assessments and a CT, with short term memory loss diagnosed. It was thought to be linked to a lacunar stroke reported on CT. My cousin had also managed to raise an ACAT (Aged Care Assessment Team) consultation.

Whilst waiting on this news, I researched to understand the condition, but soon stopped reading medical journals that explained Alzheimer's disease stages, chronicling in detail, the inevitable decline into persistent vegetative state. Instead I read a really helpful non-medical book called 'Contented Dementia' by Oliver James [4]. It offered a compelling case for improving a dementia sufferer's wellbeing by meeting them at their perception of the world rather than challenging them. Challenging their perception only serves to undermine them, whilst meeting at their capacity improves their confidence. When I did manage to get over to Oz, I wanted to be in a place of knowing how to be, to best support him. At this point I went upstairs to (hopefully) catch a few hours' sleep. Sam echoed my bewilderment at how much had changed for us in the last 14 hours, even if it was a good thing that it was moving so quickly. Later that morning, I received another shock when I spoke with Dad.

When my parents travelled in their caravan, it wasn't unusual for them to go off the grid for calls, so I hadn't seen him in a few months. From last seeing a happy, engaged chatty guy, to this old guy searching for words and concepts in basic conversation was heart-breaking. This is a man who read the entire works of Shakespeare in his youth and helped me with my high school algebra, trigonometry and advanced calculus. Thank goodness for that little selfie window on my laptop. I could keep checking my facial expression from showing my upset. Instead, I was able to keep an expression of interest, as if it were totally normal to take so long to arrange a sentence that made little sense. Mum sat by his side, patiently encouraging him to continue. In answer to a question from Mum, I replied that I had been in contact with Alex. 'What were you talking about?' Dad asked, lighting up a bit, as if to catch me out. 'Just arranging visits….' I replied. Then sensing that he deserved more honesty, and to assess his level of insight I added, '…and about your health and wellbeing.' He replied sweetly, with a smile, 'But I'm getting better.' I gulped and nodded returning his smile, taking some small comfort in his placidity and lack of insight.

Lunch was planned the next day with Sarah and for the first time since our disagreement, I was invited. After this latest news, I was relaxed with whatever unfolded. Forgiveness, I read somewhere, is more than letting go of the past, but being with that person in a way that wipes the slate clean. As things were, before it ever happened. That's how it was when we caught up with Sarah that Christmas. I got to see her for the funny, engaging young lady that she is. I met Sarah for the first time as an adult in her own right, without any investment in how she should or shouldn't be and she was delightful. We polished a couple of G+Ts over lunch at a charming restaurant of her choosing and it was nice for me to not think about the situation with Dad for an hour or so. Just to talk fun, light-hearted stuff. At the end of our catch up, Sarah went to hug me, as Sam went to hug her and so we all laughed and had a warm, 3-way embrace.

Meanwhile, the family plan in Oz was underway. Olivia and Seth urged Karen to suggest to Mum that she stay and settle in the area. There were more family and better medical facilities in the Hunter region (north of Sydney), compared with Rockhampton. The GP discharged Dad on the basis of the CT and Mum was simply advised to cue his memory. With his complex presentation, I wondered if he should be receiving a consultation with a geriatrician. Before I had time to question this, ACAT made the same suggestion. Whilst they fed this back to the GP, it gave me the time to research the set up locally.

It turned out that the Hunter had a world class set up for dementia care because of the joined up service. I managed to locate a contact for the GP to refer to, which she was happy to do. After that I took a conscious step back from his medical care. Especially with a centre of excellence, I could trust the experts. They eventually confirmed the diagnosis of Alzheimer's and as such, it was more important that energies were focussed on this being as happy and peaceful a time as possible for Mum and Dad.

Seth, who has always been an on the ball admin ninja, co-ordinated all applications for subsidies relating to moving and found a rental property. He also put the caravan into his warehouse storage, arranged the repairs through Mum's insurer and put it on the market. Together with Olivia, they were an unstoppable force. They scoured gumtree, freecycle and eBay for home furnishing bargains. Olivia, who has an interior design background, absolutely excelled in furnishing the house to look like a modern but comfortable home. Everything was considered and on moving in, assisted by Alex too, the place looked as if they had been living there for ages.

In April, I received a message from Olivia regarding some over the top spending on Mum's card statements, which couldn't be sustained. She suggested that we needed a family intervention. This was a difficult situation, because we knew that she'd had a history of this kind of spending and it was Dad that used to (try to) control it. I've never thrown money at the problem, but have on more than one occasion, helped them rearrange their finances when things were spiralling out of control. It was probably the case that Mum's old habits would surface under this kind of pressure. The problem was that there were no documented incidences from the past.

Without evidence, it would be difficult to go down the legal route to declare her unfit to manage the finances. Sam agreed that there was little we could do, aside appeal to Mum and help if she would admit to problem spending. I mentioned that Olivia had contacted me with her concerns, and as I half expected, Mum denied it. She said, 'Olivia is just overreacting, and I told her to mind her own business. Who is the mum and who is the daughter anyway?' she said angrily. 'There's nothing to worry about.' I wasn't entirely reassured, but I saw little else that we could do at that point.

The main concern which we may be able to influence, was the crazy slow progress on getting support in place for mum. Mum was looking increasingly tired and all that had been put into place, was physio for her shoulders, a carer to visit half a day a week and a social worker. Several attempts to email the social worker continued to bounce, despite Mum supplying the address a number of times. I resigned to being able to do no more until I arrived as planned, in November.

That was until one Sunday in July. During a video call, Mum snapped at Dad in a fashion that appeared unprovoked. 'That's it, I'm leaving home,' she said angrily. Dad, with a sad face and eyes, said sweetly, 'Can I come with you?' It took every ounce of control not to lose it in front of them. Not to shout, 'Don't speak to my dad like that!' I completed the call and took a breath. After stepping back and talking it over with Sam, I decided to phone Mum back from a more composed place. From a perspective of being genuinely concerned that this behaviour was symptomatic of compassion fatigue.

'I'm concerned about you Mum,' I shared, 'I see your manner with Dad, and I wonder if you might be burning out?' Mum explained that earlier that day they were at a party with Filipino family. As per usual on social occasions, he would have a few more beers than was sensible for his digestion. He failed to respond to Mum's requests to stop drinking or to change his bag. Once it was too late, there was an accident all over Auntie Nennie's nice bathmat. 'Aunt Nen was okay about it, but not all the cousins understand, and it was very embarrassing.' 'Now I understand,' I replied. 'I do care,' she said. 'Mum, it didn't cross my mind once to think otherwise,' I affirmed.

She then described watching a programme the other evening about drug addiction and Dad made some offhand comment, like, 'They should get a grip.' To which Mum replied, 'Where's your compassion? These people have an illness like you do… but you're never going to get better.' She started to cry as he held her in his arms and said, 'I know.' She cried again on relating the story. It's the first time she had cried in front of me about his illness and my tears flowed too. 'None of this is made easier by having virtually no break from this,' I added, 'There must be more resources available to cover more respite than one half day a week. Please, promise me you'll make it a priority to get more support arranged.'

When we spoke the next week, Mum had been busy. She phoned ACAT and they suggested a link that she could access for a login, to view the case assessment and codes authorised for funding. Mum said, 'I played dumb and she printed them off for me and posted them.' 'Well played,' I said, 'your charm has always been a real asset.' It was impressive how much had been approved, nursing, cleaning, overnight respite at home or in a care home.

'You could have Dad in overnight and eventually phase him into the best place, so that he would know no different.' Mum's face told me that this comment was too soon. Mum was raised in a village where they looked after their elders. Despite pointing out that elders in the Philippines were unlikely to live long enough to develop western conditions like Alzheimer's, Mum was having none of it.

The experience of spending a month in a home whilst her collarbone healed, had made up her mind. She didn't want to put him into a place like that. I explained that her experience of the home, having full faculties of mind would be very different to someone who has dementia. That it would be sensible to at least sound out options and find out which facilities would suit his care needs with the luxury of time, rather than to wait for an emergency situation, as I had seen many times in my career. For example, if he was to fall, break his hip and wasn't deemed to be fit to return back home, a nursing home would be chosen under time pressure. Better to have the information to hand and not to need it, than be in a situation of needing it and not having it. Then the choice is taken away. She clearly wasn't ready to even entertain the idea hypothetically, by the stony facial expression, silence and change of subject. I pulled back, thinking that perhaps planting the seed would make it easier when the disease progression necessitates a move. She would also know that she has my blessing.

6th October 2018

The signal from our apartment on holidays was too poor to receive a video call, so Mum sent the following message:

Okay i have to tell you that i have been to hospital for suspected heart attack im okay now. it happen at 4.20 am this morning. they sent me home at 10.30 am.i got to see the gp for more investigation by specialist. don't worry im okay. love and miss lots. mum.xxxoooo

'I think I'm going to stop going on holidays,' I said to Sam. 'The only upshot is that you're allowed to have Sangria here at lunchtime.' When I was able to speak with Mum, she described lying in the hospital bed, thinking on the inevitability of having to arrange for her husband to go into care. Whilst she signed up for better or worse, she couldn't get ill for him. It wouldn't be fair to do that to the kids, she thought. 'Whilst I don't think that I'm stressed by this situation, my body must be.'

This insight was the biggest blessing that came from this cardiac episode. I was due to land in a month and this saved the scenario of having to conflict with her regards the plan. I explained that transition into care shouldn't be seen as a failure.

Aiming for a smooth transition into residential, should be the goal. There comes a time where institutionalised support by trained carers is in their best interests. 'I just don't want anyone to think badly of me,' she said. 'Mum,' I said gently, 'making this decision is a show of strength and kindness. It's because you love him that you have to do this. I don't think badly of you and If anyone does, they don't understand the situation. Besides, I don't want to lose you to illness too.'

Chapter 11
Car crash

4th November 2018

I woke up at 5am this morning in floods of tears, of pure gratitude to wake up at all. The evening before, I was driving out of London on the northbound motorway in the outside lane, when breaking through my consciousness in a sudden moment, I saw the brake lights of the car in front. As I went to apply my brakes, I saw smoke coming out of their tyres. I remember slamming on and my car juddering as the wheels tried to grip the road, so I pulled off the brakes a little, afraid of skidding, as I accepted that I was going to hit. A muted thud - and then silence for a moment.

I ran a quick check over myself and felt fine except for the tiniest bit of chest bruising. Then I leap straight out of the car to check on the folks in front. Eric, a tall guy in a smart long trench suit coat, was tending to his wife in the passenger seat. I shouted, 'Is everyone okay?'. Eric was too occupied to answer.

I then saw a mum and 2 children at the next car in front. The kids were almost hysterical with crying and their mum just kept shouting, 'A lorry hit us and he just went off!!! He just drove away!!' I asked her, 'Are you okay, are your kids okay?' They seemed shaken but physically fine. Mum and Sanjay, their dad, were holding and comforting their little boy and girl.

I went back and asked Eric if his wife was okay as she was still sitting in their car, clearly in pain. 'Is she okay?' I asked again. 'Yes,' he said finally, but just hurt from the seatbelt. It wasn't surprising with the damage to the front of their car, crushing the BMW's bonnet in half. Looking at the damage to the back of the front car (a smaller Peugeot), I'm surprised that the children were actually uninjured. I started to notice how cold it was and went back to the mum to see if anyone needed any coats. The question prompted her to open her crumpled boot and replied, 'Thank you, but we have some in here.' Sanjay dived into action to retrieve supplies for his family.

I asked Eric, if we should we phone the police? He said, 'Yeah, I'll sort it.' I looked at my car; both head lights were still on, though the one on the passenger side was dented into the bumper. The front fender was gone so that I could see my radiator. I could hear the horns of motorists behind us, so I jumped into my car to put my hazards on and to my surprise, could start the engine, so I drove it to the hard shoulder.

Eric told me that they had located us from an aerial view and the police were on their way. Sanjay couldn't find his phone. His wife was calming down and sweetly asked me if I wanted some chocolate. I said thank you so much but politely declined. I was honestly touched, but was trying to stay off sugar, having just attended a nutrition seminar all day. She insisted, 'We have spare and you have a long way to travel.' I was 140 miles from home, but I'm sure that I had enough adrenalin running, that a dose of caffeine and sugar were the last thing I needed. 'Thank you honestly, it's very kind of you, but I'm fine.' Soon after this, she brought her little girl across who offered me a small packet of Maltesers with the most beautiful brown eyes peering from her fluffy jacket hood. Her mum said, 'She wants you to have this.' How could I refuse, 'Aw thank you sweetie.'

I tried for the 5th or 6th time to phone Sam, but there was no answer. He's not great with phones, but somehow, I was fine with this and realised that I would just have to rely on my resources. I was amazed at how calm I was when I spoke with

149

my insurer, but was also aware that I wasn't thinking completely straight, as the information was coming out a bit jumbled in order. I was able to piece together the story with the help of the other drivers. Sanjay's Peugeot was pushed from left to right - from the 3rd to the 4th lane into the path of Eric's BMW. We considered that the lorry could have been a left-hand drive, so might not have seen or felt the small car. As I explained this to the very calm and helpful insurance company guy, he reassured me that because I had no claims protection, the good news was that it won't affect my premium. The good news was that we were all still alive….

The cars had to be towed by a company nominated by the Highway's Agency to get us off the motorway as soon as possible and would remain at junction 12. Eric gave me a big hug as we left the scene. I'll never forget the kindness and humanity between us all. Absolutely everyone from the Police, the Highways guys, the Paramedics and the Recovery tow truck drivers were so kind and reassuring; keeping it all light-hearted. I could feel my ribs hurting from laughing, but it felt good to laugh. I didn't mention my ribs, because from my background, I knew that I was fine and didn't want to draw attention in my mind to any pain so that it would pass more quickly, without fear.

With my car in impound, a recovery van couldn't be called by my insurer, so the best option was to get a taxi from the depot to the nearest hotel. Although I felt wired, I figured sleep was a better option over picking up a hire car that night. I was on my way to a glass of red and a bath when I got hold of Sam on the phone. 'I'm ok, honestly,' I told him. 'I have a little bruising in my ribs, but I'm absolutely fine.' I related the story with a level head until I described seeing the 2 kids crying with their mum by the roadside. They seemed such a loving family. The emotion broke through at this point, my voice trembled, and tears welled up. I put my hand over my mouth on recalling my fears of how much worse it could have been.

The enormity of it all hit as I woke up next morning. I walked out of this. I'm here. I'm so grateful to be here. The sheer volume of emotion choked my sobs into my duvet there in the hotel. How great is my life? How thankful that I am to keep living it? The purpose to make the most of it was renewed. I resolved to ask God as often as I remember, 'How can I serve?' I want for nothing. Only to give and serve.

I was flying to Australia that night to spend 10 days with my folks. Dad's Alzheimer's was deteriorating to a level where Mum was seriously struggling to cope. I had it in mind to provide support, to organise services and to get a plan in place . for Mum. To spend quality time with Dad, but up until this moment, I still wasn't exactly clear on how I would be. Now it was crystal. I wanted to let Dad know that he needn't ever worry about his welfare – 'We will always have your best interests at heart. We've got you and I've got Mum. Sam's got me.' All the petty squabbles with my siblings or the trepidation on how to deal with them vanished in a moment. I'm alive. I have this chance.

I found a deeper clarity to see how I had conditions on life. Expectations that things and people should be a certain way. I finally saw this and understood that I can let everyone be from a place of observation, like being in the world but not of it. To not get caught up and reactive. Before this experience, these ideas were just words. From that moment I could be truly grateful for every moment in my life and all that happens without judging situations as good or bad. I have at times behaved like such a righteous arse in pointing out to people when I see them as falling short. As if it was somehow my duty to help them see this, to help them grow.

The worst part of this fault finding was that I felt justified doing this from a 'place of love' and then wondered why it wasn't well received. As though, because I had been more giving, that I somehow had the right to point out that they weren't holding up their end in the relationship. Often from a martyr space I would serve up a hefty dose of guilt on the side. I don't have the insight to see the whole picture or how things should turn out. I can let life carry me and just keep asking, 'How can I best serve during my time here… on this little rock.' I couldn't wipe the smile off my face. I phoned Sam on a coffee stop on the way home, 'You know how it is when you've used one of your lives and just feel grateful and nothing else matters… I don't want this feeling to stop!'

This chapter was written on the plane, in an effort to stay awake for the first leg. Currently over Germany, with 35,060-foot views over life and with 10 hours and 56 minutes until I touch down in Singapore. For the first time in all my years of flying, I intended to enjoy the experience, instead of viewing it as a drudgery, a stage to be endured. I never want to view a single minute of my life that way. I intend, as much as possible to live in the present moment, mindfully breathing through my life with intention and purpose.

From the moment I collided with that car, I could never be the same. I drew a line under old tendencies and shifted towards patience and non-judgement, with gratitude for moment to moment awareness of things as they are; without the urge to fix or change them. On the road, the option of slowing down rather than overtaking, is a choice that brings a more peaceful, mindful, aware, open state with a broader perspective.

I reflected that this tendency to find fault and point it out to others, maybe came from my job of 'fixing pain.' What started as a well-intended motivation to help and heal, became a fault-finding negative habit that crept into my relationships. 'I understand you', became 'I understand *what is wrong with you*' – as Steve Covey put it, this is a substitute for true empathy [2]. 'Fixing pain' or 'healing' isn't actually my job anyway. If I flip it, I could see my role as augmenting the best of what works and facilitate people to work on their strengths. In doing so I can have a much more positive framework of viewing the world. Rather than looking to 'fix' anything, I resolved to listen, understand and signpost Mum and Dad to find a solution that suits them. After all, I'll be there in person for just 10 days and even if I were able to stay longer, they still have to own the solution.

"Gratitude is not only the greatest of virtues,

but the parent of all others" Cicero.

Chapter 12

Family memories

I'm so glad that I made transfers from Sydney easy. I booked a shuttle straight from the airport to Mum and Dad's front door. The Melbourne Cup was on that afternoon, so there was enough time to freshen up and head for drinks at the local bowling club. We met up with Aunty Silvia. 'You look just the same!' I said as I hugged her. 'I'm a bit wider than when I saw you last time lovie. Can hardly get out of a chair these days with this big bum.' I love my Aussie family. The jetlag clouds my memory of which horse I backed and if anyone had picked the winner, but it was just nice to chill in great company even if I was only semi-alert.

After a Skype call with Sam, I joined Mum, Dad and Alex in the living room. In conversation that first night, there was an opening to discuss Dad's condition. He spoke openly and expressed a real insight and level of acceptance. Dad noted that he been aware of some difficulty in staying with conversation threads for many years. Despite now being aware of the diagnosis, he took things day-to-day, moment to moment. He told me that he gained this skill from two experiences in his life. One, facing his mortality in surviving cancer and the second, being on a boat, off Papua New Guinea when for a whole week, they didn't know whether they would live or die. 'So, it takes some practice,' he advised, but he has come to a place where he can stay present. Mum broke in at that point and said, 'It's not like that for me. I'm not coping as well at that,' and she walked out of the room. I let her go. There'll be more time to explore that later.

The next afternoon, I caught up for a big family get together in the park. It was so lovely. By the water, the band played every Friday, weather permitting. There were so many folks to catch up with, that I felt like a proper social butterfly. It was great, there were cousins that I hadn't met in years I made a beeline for Auntie Thelma and gave her a huge hug, saying into her ear, 'I'm so glad to see you Aunty Thelly! As a Brit you're the only one who understands me when I say, that there's no decent gin and tonic in this town.' She hugged me closer and said in her lovely Somerset accent, 'Oh my Darlin', I will always understand you.'

My cousin Kath pulled my ponytail to interrupt. She couldn't wait to say, 'What's with your mum?! Why didn't she call us when she had that heart attack?! Seth was hours away and we're just up the road! If I was at work, Michael is available or Karen. One of us would have been there to watch over your dad. 'I know, I've already told her off about that. She's crazy proud and doesn't want to burden you guys. I know it's not like that because he's your Uncle too. I'll kick her but again for ya.' 'Dad's pretty content, it's Mum who's carrying the stress,' I shared with Gary, who works with dementia. 'I know. He's super chilled, but your mum is going up the bloody wall!' He then pointed to his wife Karen and said, 'Just contact her. She's the matriarch, the shepherd. When she puts her staff in the ground and all will round up.'

On talking with Mum about this, she said that if it wasn't for the stoma, she would rely more on the family, but with the way he stubbornly refuses to change his bag in time, 'I couldn't put that on them.' So, getting more professional respite sounded like the solution. I was amazed that there was only one half-day a week in place at present, but it had been hard to understand the process from the UK. In prep for the meeting with the social worker next morning, I was able to get my head around the situation. Mum was appointed case manager, whilst awaiting the care package to come through on a waiting list.

It's understandable that she was struggling with this arrangement. The services authorised by government codes, are provided privately and not all companies cover all services. Mum held 3 separate contracts. Without having ever dealt with government, unable to operate a web search or send emails, English being her second language and being in the process of grieving over her husband's illness; appointing Mum the case manager, explained why getting services in place was grinding so slowly.

By the time Daniela, the social worker arrived, I was able to untangle most of the admin and generate some files on my laptop. It would have been easy to launch in with questioning why everything was taking so long and start pushing for her to be more accountable / set some timeframes etc. Instead I started with sharing how highly Mum speaks of her (which was true) and thanked her for her assistance to date. From this I learned of the difficulties that she was facing and that she was doing an amazing job. Daniela attended a GP session to ensure that the paperwork was completed correctly for the purpose of funding. 'They're often just very busy and don't understand the terms to put in, but if you plant the seed....' we said the second part of the sentence together, 'like it's their idea,' 'and make their life easy, ' I smiled, 'you get the job done.' We high fived.

'How's your wrist Daniela?' Mum asked. 'It's ok thanks, but I still get this aching up the forearm now and then.' I wouldn't normally get involved in this context, but she had stepped up and over for Mum, so I asked a few questions and examined her wrist. It seemed a pretty straight forward case of adverse neurodynamics post distal radial fracture which was confirmed healed, so I advised her on some gentle neural mobility work, complete with warnings and the get out of jail advice to contact her GP if it hasn't settled in a week and ask for a physio referral.

Once we were clear on the plan, Mum mentioned that she was off to see her cardiologist in a few days, but that she expected it would just be to rule things out. Mum thought it was stress. Daniela agreed that it's good to rule these things out, not just for safety but also to reduce the anxiety surrounding it. Because of her psychology background she was able to give the best explanation of fight or flight stress mechanisms that I've ever heard. I felt calmer after participating in a breathing exercise designed to talk the body down from a high alert state.

Sadly, the effect wasn't to last long. I spoke with Olivia that afternoon, 'So are you coming to Sydney? The boys would love to see their Aunty Jules.' She wanted me to come to her place in Sydney inner west, as Erin was due to have his surgery for complication from his sepsis. 'With everything that you're going through, might it be not be wiser to meet up next time?' I suggested. 'No, really,' she insisted. If you can come to ours, we would love to catch up.' I explained how wiped out and slightly traumatised I was, off the back of the crazy car crash of a departure from the UK. 'I'm not sure that the boys would want to meet a crazy Auntie Jules.'

I wondered why I felt it necessary to offer up an elaborate story to justify not travelling to her location. I had managed to decline catching up with several friends who all understood that my focus of energy had to be with my parents. Whilst all that I said was true, she was the only one that I babbled on to about being traumatised and having problems sleeping.

'Honey I'm so sorry to hear that,' she said, making some helpful suggestions regards nutritional supplements. She added that, 'We can have a chilled-out time and the kids will just be happy to see you however you are.' 'Olivia,' I replied, 'I'm not being funny, but they're not likely to remember me in a year or two.' I immediately regretted that remark as soon as it came out, for how harsh it sounded. 'I'm so exhausted and on the edge of it, that I've gotta be gentle with myself and travelling to yours then onto Rhodes to stay with my friend is just going to finish me off. Let's leave it to next time.' I could hear my voice take on an uncharacteristic begging tone. 'They remember more than you think.... It's about establishing *family* memories.' She emphasised the word *family* with an angry sounding tone. I made my excuses to get off the phone, saying that we'll talk about it later.

They say friends are family that you choose for yourself. I would have loved to catch up with my soul sister Lindsay, but she lived in Queensland and I didn't want her to commit flying down especially, only to find that I hardly had any time because of the family situation. Tessa had recently moved to Rhodes in Sydney and offered for me to stop over if I had time. Tessa knew just what to say when I first received the news of Dad's dementia. No clichés, no advice, just a couple of anecdotes from her time in aged care, which illustrated the beauty and innocence of those with the condition. Despite working with elite dancers and circus performers for most of her career, she maintained that some of her most rewarding times were with those senior folks.

Erin's mum also lived in Rhodes. Perhaps Olivia and family (if Erin was feeling up to it) could travel the 15-minute drive from their house. It seemed like the perfect solution. It would cut transit through Sydney Central out for me. No transfer to a light rail or walking in the heat, with a trolley bag, again. I texted through the idea. Erin's mum was up for it, but Olivia instead offered to drive me back to their nearest train station if I could come to her house. The old 'people pleasing' me would have gone along with this, especially because of Erin's health situation, but I was at peace with the fact that a 24-hour flight and 2 hours on the train was as far as I was prepared to meet her. To her offer I replied, No thanks. 'Perhaps let's meet next time Olivia x'. She decided to meet me in Rhodes.

I was ready to turn it in when Alex approached for a chat. I've learned that it's best to take up these opportunities to connect with him when they arise, as they can be few and far between, so I grabbed a glass of red, smiled and genuinely said, 'Of course.' We chatted the night into the morning, mostly about his life and he confessed that I was too much of an extrovert for him to cope with at times. Instead of taking the comment personally, I decided to appreciate his honesty. I explained that some of this is the sleep deprivation but agreed to try and settle down. I warned him though that despite my best efforts, Mum, also a bubbly extrovert, could get me going and if this disturbs his peace, I wouldn't be offended if he stepped out of our company for time out.

On a walk to the waterfront next day, we found a subject that engaged Dad and made him feel an expert. Oliver James writes in Contented Dementia, that finding such a subject is gold [4]. As we approached a boat moored up at the pier, I jokingly said, 'Let's take a photo by this boat Dad and I can tell everyone at work that you bought this one for me.' He lit up talking about his sailing days in Papua New Guinea. His walking pace picked up, seemingly oblivious of the distance he was covering. Mum eventually started looking a little tired of his sailing days monologue and Dad's walking slowed a little, so I took the opportunity to sit them both down at a park bench and entertain. I co-ordinated Dad's story to yoga moves. I enjoyed a good stretch from hours of sitting on the plane and in front of my laptop.

'Did he jump off like this?' I asked, leap frogging in the air. 'Not quite,' Dad said, playing along and Mum laughing. 'How about this then?' I bounced off a tree. 'That's more like it,' smiled Dad. He may go back to his sailing adventures more and more as his other memory maps fade and walking to see the boats might be the solution to the daily struggle of getting Dad out for a walk as the Doctors recommended.

After dinner we got talking about Dad's tendency to sneak in more treats than he should with his diabetes. I described the consequences of poorly controlled diabetes, which he nodded to in agreement, without looking at all engaged. I stepped it up a notch from vision issues to amputation. Still not bothered. It felt like it was a game to him to appear to be listening yet remaining unperturbed. In frustration I said, 'Fine. It's your choice Dad, sorry for caring. It's your life.' He appeared amused and replied, 'That's ok sweetie,' I excused myself from the table and said angrily, 'I'm off to bed, I'm way too tired to continue this chat.'

'Not too tired for a chat with me I hope?' Alex, who wanted time out that evening and ate his dinner on the back porch, had resurfaced at 11pm to re-connect. 'Way too tired Alex,' I snapped. I had reached my limit indulging him too. He angrily started shouting that I told him that it was fine to have time out and, 'Now that I'm ready,' I shouted louder than him to complete his sentence 'It's now my time to be alone!' I left the room and took his spot outside. As I went to walk out, I saw Mum's face distraught with tears welling up and realised that I was going to have to cool it. Mum joined me outside to share Alex's perspective, which was that I was cutting in on his time to just chill with his dad. Rather than escalate things by pointing out how little time I have in this country, I did my best to see it from his perspective.

If there was sibling rivalry, it wouldn't be surprising. He told me that he had been there for days under a world war 3 atmosphere with the folks, then I arrive to a prodigal daughter reception and everyone was on their 'better' behaviour. I decided to get out of his way and contacted Tessa to sound out if I could spend 2 nights at hers. It would be easier on me to land into Rhodes the day before I catch up with Olivia and family in any case. Tessa was of course delighted with the revised plan.

The next morning, I cried in the shower about the loss of my Dad's beautiful personality. I cried tears of rage at him being taken away before I got to say goodbye. He had been replaced with a stubborn child in a man's body. No impulse control around socialisation or food. Like a child, he had to be the centre of conversation and most tragically had lost his empathy. I reasoned that his struggle for power was understandable. He was being stubborn about bag changes, because he was holding onto the last thing that he can control. He even said in Mum's presence, 'She knows that she has the upper hand now.' He managed a department of auditors for a living. Now he can't even drive a car. He just won't be told what to do. He appears to agree, whilst getting his way, especially when the other person loses the plot.

I tested my theory out the next time he stalled on a bag change. His reply to Mum's third request was, 'I told you, I'll do it when

I've finished this coffee.' She protested that he had been sitting on that coffee for 20 minutes and the smell was making her ill. No good appealing to his empathy I thought, let's give him a rise. 'Dad, give us a look at that coffee.' He handed it over and I walked to the sink acting a little angry and poured it out. 'Now you're done.' He laughed to himself and went off to change.

Amongst ourselves, Mum and I described him as a 'shell'. A man walking around in my Dad's body with none of the features of his personality. In fact, this person has been swapped to someone of an entirely opposite personality. My Dad had been replaced by someone with a covert personality disorder. He could put on a sweet agreeable front in social circles, and behind closed doors, do his best to press his loved ones' buttons in a game of passive aggressive resistance. 'My dad' would have really disliked this man and the way that he was treating his closest family. I asked Mum to count the number of years that she had 'Dad as we knew him.' She came up with 40 years of marriage as the figure. I asked if she got a ruby ring and (half) jokingly suggested that she fund one from Dad's pension. This way of keeping it light and distancing the person from his behaviour really helped us come to terms with the grief about the personality that we lost. That although this personality wasn't behaving like him, this guy is in my Dad's body, doing the best he can with what he has and deserved care and respect.

The next day I joined Mum at the Cardiologist's. I liked the guy. I'd place him in his early seventies, with a dry sense of humour and a quick wit. He was very thorough and thoughtful in his questioning. He afforded me the time and professional courtesy to answer my questions. He performed a repeat ECG and an echocardiogram. Seeing abnormalities on both, he went all out with blood thinners, beta blockers and nitro spray. He phoned the hospital personally to see to the soonest an angiogram appointment and supplied Mum with a note to recommend that she be investigated if she was admitted with a repeat episode in the meantime. 'Don't let the paramedics talk you out of being admitted and give the hospital this letter,' he said, 'as they will be more scared of me than they are of you.' If the angiogram came back positive, on her history of diabetes, it would likely mean open heart surgery. So much for just ruling out cardiac – seems my Mum was a ticking time bomb! We had forms to fill, which we could complete over lunch and take to the hospital personally, but first up I wanted her scripts filled. 'After lunch would be fine,' Mum said. Was she just in the same consult as me? 'No Mum, let's get it now.'

On the drive back I got thinking on the implications. If open heart surgery turns out the plan, she can't be a carer for Dad. Her recovery could be compromised, and Dad's poorly managed stoma care posed an infection risk. We would have to put Dad into residential care at least on a temporary basis post op.

To put another spanner in the works, Mum then disclosed that, the finances were in trouble. In trouble was an understatement. Her maxed out loans couldn't be serviced next month. They were facing eviction and repossession of the car. She started to confess that she probably didn't help matters with... I stopped her there and said, 'Mum, it doesn't matter how you got here, let's just work a solution.' We recorded all the figures down on a spreadsheet and phoned a debt helpline service. The concern now was that moving Dad into care at this time would cancel her carers allowance and Mum would not be able to meet the bills. They were still in contract on their accommodation lease. Crap. This called for a glass of heart healthy red and Tom Jones karaoke to let off a bit of steam.

Mum and I held our party on the back porch, because Dad's really not a fan of ol' Tom. I remember Mum having an equally strong dislike of Dad's favourite Nanna Maskouri records, so for the sake of truce, neither artist got much airtime growing up at home. In this new context though, Dad seemed blissfully unaware, content inside with his telly turned up.

After a couple of tunes, we got chatting and Mum opened up about her relationship with Seth. That a while back, she asked for forgiveness for how harshly she had treated him as a child. 'He just happened to be there at a time when I was in a difficult place. Not that this was an excuse, but he deserved an explanation.' She took him aside for a chat one to one as she wanted her apology to be heartfelt and meaningful. 'That's good,' I affirmed. 'When he asked for my forgiveness, it was really off hand, like, 'Sorry about that.' I think he may have felt too awkward.' I had already forgiven him anyway. 'How did he respond to your apology?' I asked. 'He said at least now I understand.' Seth being there for Mum in her vulnerability at this time may heal some things between them.

The next morning, I managed to tiptoe out of a sleeping house to escape for a run. I found the most serene path alongside a lake, complete with lily pads, reeds, ducks and ducklings. Mist was floating over the water and it was so still and peaceful. Just the rhythm of my feet and the sound of my breathing. In each moment, breath by breath; taking in the fresh morning air each inhale and letting go each exhale, letting the beauty of my surroundings in more each breath. I always feel like everything's better after a run.

Mum's Physio was running late for her home visit and we couldn't be sure how long, so I went ahead and prepared breakfast for everyone. Of course, she arrived just as it was served. 'Please guys go ahead,' she said, apologising for the delay. 'If you tuck in Mum, would you mind if I had a quick chat with Shannon?' 'Sure,' they both said. I informed my colleague of the possibility of Mum's heart surgery. 'Oh dear,' Shannon said, 'your mum is the most motivated patient ever, so she'll recover well.' 'Yeah,' I agreed 'she has a really positive attitude and is super keen on getting back to golf too.' That afternoon I stayed out of the way during the treatment but could hear Mum thwack a couple of balls, followed by laughter as her aim needed a little work. They narrowly missed the garage window!

There was a café in town which my family frequented for brunch. I gave Alex and Dad the chance to opt out, which they took. My cousin Mike asked, 'Where are the other two?' I told him how Alex was feeling a little cut out from spending time with Dad, so we left them to it. We also did the same for afternoon tea with Mum's cousin Nenni and her husband Uncle Brent. It would be easier for Mum too, to have some time out from worrying about Dad's behaviour at social occasions. It was great to see them both. I was a teenager when I saw them last. It was also great to see Mum and Aunt Nenni talk about times in the Philippines when they were teenagers. Nenni was the good student and Mum was the bad influence. I could definitely see that one playing out!

On the journey back home, Mum asked me to make things up with Alex. 'I have every intention to Mum,' I replied, 'but I won't indulge poor behaviour. I can't be the person that I used to be. I'm no longer a doormat and won't apologise for who I am, but I'm also about peace.'

I was heading to Rhodes the next day and Alex was leaving for home the day after, so it was our last night together. We all watched a movie of Alex's choice and I committed to keeping quiet, which wasn't difficult due to being absolutely shattered. I hope he didn't notice me snoozing on the sofa during the movie! He supplied the wine and cooked dinner for us that evening, which was very thoughtful.

The next morning, I waited for him to strike up conversation so as to not seem overbearing. We had some time chatting until it was time for him to go to work. We hugged and I said that I'm so happy for him that he seemed well and to just keep doing what he's doing (we covered in our heart to heart a couple of nights ago, that his life was working well). He said, 'Yep. That's the plan,' with a tone of irritation. I physically stepped back, with an open 'hands-off' gesture and apologised. 'Sorry, you're right. You've got this.' I waved goodbye, but more importantly, I said farewell to the perception of a baby brother, in need of caretaking.

It was a stunning train journey along the Hawkesbury river and surrounding countryside. I had been navigating emotional landmines with Alex and trying to be the buffer between my folks for a week now. Sam was the most amazing support and I was able to clear my head every night over Skype whilst everyone slept, thanks (or perhaps no thanks) to my body clock still being on UK time. I packed my training kit as I had only managed one run out and was determined for at least one more from Tessa's place.

I arrived before Tessa finished work and so walked around the local shopping mall in search of gifts for the boys and practice golf balls for Mum. It was great to just be shopping on my own and it reminded me of a mall that I used to shop in as a teenager. On the way out, I clocked the location of Erin's mum's and then stopped for a coffee at a cafe en route to Tessa's. It was not only for more 'me time,' but I couldn't shake the military habit of doing a reconnaissance mission. Sam would be proud. Perfect for a catch up with my primary school buddy Adam tomorrow. Easy road access - check, parking – check, water views, a reasonable menu and an unpretentious atmosphere, with good coffee – check, check.

Tessa gave huge hugs in greeting me to her fab apartment. All the cool furniture had come from her apartment in Canada. Despite looking fairly unpacked, she had only been there a week and I was her first visitor. Showing up a day early threw a spanner in the works, as on top of unpacking, she had hit the ground running with business meetings in Sydney and Melbourne. She could cook tomorrow, 'but would sushi do tonight?' she asked apologetically. 'Would sushi do tonight?' I mocked, 'Are you kidding? I live in the sticks in Yorkshire now, and any opportunity for sushi is amazing!' We washed it down with Spanish bubbly just like Barcelona and laughed about our international reunions. Adelaide, London, Glasgow, Barcelona, Sydney. Cheers.' Your mum phoned earlier to check whether you'd arrived, and I thanked her for sharing her Jules. She replied with the most amazing expression of unconditional love – 'Jules is so precious, how could I not share her with the world?'

After a morning run to blow off the Spanish bubbles, I hit the shower and headed to the café. I've known Adam since I was 5 years old and he was the one who was always there to help me move my stuff out, when the bust ups with boyfriends in my 20's landed. He grew up with my family too, so as extended family, I wanted to update him in person. He has a great dry sense of humour and we somehow found a way to have a proper belly laugh about the way this crazy family story had unfolded. I can't even remember the last time we met up; years for sure. His little boy had started school now and he wasn't even a dad back then, so at least 5 years. 'Shame you couldn't meet Myles today.' Adam had snuck out of work to meet, 'but maybe you can come to his graduation.' 'Haha! Maybe,' I agreed. It felt like no time at all since we last caught up.

Next, I was off to meet my adorable nephews. Jimmy was into space travel and trains. Ben was just super cute and funny. I saw my sister as a loving dedicated mum, who was committed to raising her young boys into respectful young men. With respect to our history; why should I hold a grudge? The only reason that Olivia was allowed to behave like that, was because I let her. That's all in the past now and it's no longer taken personally. I'm certainly not prepared to fall out over it in future.

It was lovely to catch up with his mum, but the star of the show had to be Erin. Just days post op; he mowed the lawn yesterday! I gave him the biggest hug which was only made possible by way of nothing short of a medical miracle. I was allowed some time sipping a glass of wine with Olivia and a bite at the table, before I was kidnapped by the boys for a football match downstairs. Not sure you could call Auntie Jules' skills football, but they were entertained.

Tessa was changing styles from Barcelona chic to Sydney business, so I was happy to help give her kit from a past life, a new home. Over a fantastic prawn curry and more cava of course, we had a fashion show and painted my nails to match the outfit that I had picked for tomorrow's meeting. I had lined up a 2nd meeting for my return, with Daniela and included Karen. Mum was fine to be absent and for me to relay any information but asked that I keep the financials from Karen. Mum was afraid that Karen, being so generous, may offer to help. I put Tessa on the phone for a chat to Mum on loudspeaker. 'Hi Mum,' said Tessa. I'm having a great time with Jules. We had an emergency plumber drop by to fix a water leak and she tried to get his number for me.' 'Why don't you date Seth, my son,' Mum replied. 'He just lives up the road from you.' Tessa didn't see me flinch.

As we were about to head out for breakfast next morning, the subject of Seth came up. I tried to put her off. 'Why not?' she teased, 'better the devil you know.' I was just going to have to out and say it. I shared the short version of a story that I've told very few people and she looked shocked. I think she was too stunned to say much and so we headed out for breakfast in silence. After some time, I asked, 'Did I upset you? I've had so much time processing this myself that I sometimes forget how unsettling it is for others to hear.' 'No my sweetie,' she replied, 'you can tell me anything.' She linked arms with me as we headed to the café.

Over breakfast, the coffee had me racing on with the details of all the things that I wanted to cover in the meeting. Tessa held my arm as if to say, stop! 'This is your last night with your folks tonight and my worry for you is…' 'That I'll miss it?' I asked, completing her sentence. My face looked way too sober, and she opened her mouth to continue. 'I get it,' I interrupted, 'It's just that I also need to keep a lid on it, because if I don't, I feel that it'll overwhelm me right now.' Tessa nodded and gave me a big farewell hug.

I picked up some flowers for Daniela and Karen because these two wonderful women had stepped over and above the call. I meditated on the train and took a cab from the station as I thought on a story that would help Mum get Dad out of the house quickly before the meeting was due to start in 30 mins. Having learned to appeal to Dad's inner child, I informed that there's a party tonight and you guys, 'have to go out and get some supplies for me.' At that, Dad sprung up and fetched his bag. Whilst Mum got ready, I checked the contents for him, as he often forgot that the spare shirt had been used. I wasn't ready for what I found.

The bag was soaked in urine. Clearly, it had been sitting next to the loo. I took a silent breath and said innocently, 'Dad this shirt is wet.' 'No it isn't,' he replied. 'Feel it,' I urged, 'See if you can get a fresh one from Mum.' Short of time, I dried the bag as best I could and lined it with plastic, replacing the stoma supplies. Poor guy, I thought. For a moment, I stepped out of being his daughter. There's one thing accepting intellectually that he needed to be in care sometime in the future. Another thing knowing emotionally and viscerally, that the time is now.

As planned, Daniela arrived first and we managed to cover the financial issues and implications, before Karen arrived. I introduced her as the amazing cousin who raised an emergency ACAT consult within 24 hours, in the week of Christmas. 'Daniela is a big fan of your work,' I said as I fixed up a teapot.

Karen was more up to speed with the codes and processes than I. This meant that I could just sit back and take notes while they worked through the best solutions. In no time we had a list of actions, which I could organise by priority on my flight.

I presented the flowers to both ladies who of course said, 'you shouldn't have!' 'I know,' I replied, 'they should be solid gold. I'm just so grateful to you both.' Daniela had to be away for her next appointment, so I showed her out and asked in passing, 'How's your wrist by the way?' 'Perfect actually,' she beamed back, waving on her way out, saying 'thanks!' I smiled back.

We did have a house party that evening. Just us three. As Tessa suggested, I put all 'fixing things' aside and just enjoyed the precious time that I had with them both.

"Treat your family like friends

and your friends like family."

Unknown.

Chapter 13

Waking up

"It is not the mountain we conquer but ourselves"

Edmund Hilary.

Wanting to stay awake for the first leg to Singapore was easy. I blew smoke off my keyboard in putting all Mum and Dad's problems into projects with contact lists and tasks. Six main problems, with plans for each, including next steps and a team of 10. This took over 10 hours to complete.

I naively thought that I could hand back at this point; and Mum, Karen and Daniela could manage it from there. Instead, the size and complexity of the problems kept growing. I took calls at all hours to collect more information and it seemed as though the more solutions I pushed through, the more arose. The more detail that I gleaned regards the finances, the more that I came to realise just how deep Mum had gotten in over her head. Her spending was completely out of control. Hitting rock bottom forced Mum to face up to her problem spending and gambling. 'It's like it's someone else,' she confessed. Seeking support brought all sorts of emotional issues to the surface and she leaned pretty heavily on me in the first few weeks of returning home to the UK.

I had also returned to a difficult work dynamic. It started from the outset 6 months ago. My colleague Peter, had little respect for boundaries on my time. When, 'This will just take a minute,' stretched onto 30 or more, on a regular basis, it was adding to the pressure. On returning tired and jetlagged, catching up on my admin was becoming more difficult. This was complicated by managing a complaint against one of our instructors and supporting one of my patients, whose lumbar scan revealed a tumour.

On absorbing that news myself first, Peter awkwardly tried to console me, by stating that it wasn't my fault. He repeated this, even when I told him that I had no concerns that anything was missed in this case. I just wanted to know if she'd be ok. I wanted to be in the right space for her when she learned the news. My practice manager was more supportive, and we rearranged the diary to give me a long weekend and catch up admin time.

I needed my top personality profiler, so that I could gain some perspective, 'Lindsay, I need your help with a colleague.' After hearing my story, she simply said, 'Jules, it sounds as though Peter's on the spectrum.' The second she suggested this, it made complete sense. We had affectionately nicknamed Peter the 'Terminator' for his uncanny ability to recall technical details and efficiently track information in the flow charts of practice guidelines. His logic was flawless when working through cases, but his communication was problematic.

It explained why others in the medical centre had been approaching me to get things done. Lindsay explained that Peter may struggle to appreciate that there are other maps of the world. 'He may see his map as the territory. Emotions are likely to be perceived as confusing and largely redundant,' she added. 'If you've managed to build rapport with him, he may have developed a fixation on you (a common behaviour) and it would explain why the boundary problems have escalated.'

When I shared this with Sam he remarked, 'That's the problem with you professionals, he's not on the spectrum, he's just a dickhead.' 'I guess that could be a layman's assessment,' I laughed, 'but labels aside, I at least have a better understanding of the relationship dynamic.'

On return from my long weekend, I felt more rested and had the patience and compassion to meet Peter where he was at. I felt ready to handle the situation with sensitivity and pragmatism, until I was thrown by Peter's outburst. In response to learning that I had arranged with the practice manager to diarise 2 half admin days, Peter shouted, 'It should never get to a situation where you need that much time to catch up! You had better get it all done by then!'

In addition to this relationship dynamic, the situation was confusing from the start. I was covering the clinical list of the head of department, but of course at my grade, not her management duties. These duties were effectively left without appointing a person responsible. Instead, the practice manager was appointed as my line manager and Peter was persuaded to take on more work. Although he was without incentive, Peter did his best to step up into the workload and delegate some to me. His communication style wasn't conducive to getting things done; yet because of my background in running a small practice, I compensated for a time. After this abuse, that time had now ended.

I went upstairs to the practice manager. 'He shouted in my face that I had better get it done!' 'Or what?' The practice manager mocked, laughing. He always had a great way of diffusing things. 'Yeah,' I shrugged, laughing along, 'or what??' He suggested that we take it to the boss to mediate.

'If the boss wants to choose the path of least resistance, he may appoint Peter as your line manager,' Sam warned. 'If so, Peter is the same grade as you; so that's something you can challenge, but with all that you have on now, I suggest you be prepared to walk away.' This echoed something that a concerned colleague and good friend said about Oz after getting me to take a breath. 'As medical folk, we often take on so much, as though it's just what we do. But this is your family and it's ok to say if it's enough.' She paused and added, '...In fact it's okay to say if it's too much.'

So that I would be factual, fair and together in expressing the issues, I wrote up the whole interaction for the boss. He read it over and discussed it with Peter. When returning to me he said,

'Peter is disappointed that things had to come to this, and I happen to agree with him.' I was a more than a little taken aback by his lack of impartiality. 'I suggest that you speak with Peter this afternoon,' he continued, 'It would be better to clear the air today, with Peter being off work tomorrow. I have a meeting to attend now, so I won't be able to join you.' ''I'd prefer that all of us meet as planned on Monday,' I replied. After all, it had gone to mediation I thought. I had little hope of things being resolved otherwise. The boss agreed to my request.

'In the meantime, can I ask something?' 'Sure,' the boss replied. The practice manager signs my time sheets, right?' 'Yes.' 'On leaving, who would write my exit report?' 'Um... I guess that would be Peter, the boss pondered for a moment, 'but I would like to have some input too,' he added quickly. Great, I have 3 managers now, I thought. 'but you don't have to worry about that because you're not going to leave and if you do, we'll give you such a bad report that you won't be able to work anywhere else.' He said this with such a dead pan expression and yet he has such a dry sense of humour that I wasn't sure whether he was kidding or not. Perhaps to him, it may have looked like I was just reactive after a tough experience in Oz. As this was the first he'd heard of any issues, he may have thought that things might blow over with a chat, making light of it and some time.

The next day was the staff Christmas party and I considered making my excuses and not attending. Then I thought, Why should I miss out? There were loads of folks I wanted to socialise with and Cassandra, the cleaner, was only going because I was. Cass and I struck up a friendship in no time. She once fretted because I attended a meeting offsite and didn't think to mention it to her. 'I was so worried about you. I thought something bad had happened when you weren't in this morning!' 'Aw Hun,' I replied, 'here's my mobile number in case you ever need to check if I'm ok.' Since then, we texted loads, because we often couldn't wait until the morning or lunch cleaning rounds to catch up.

Of course, the first two to arrive at the Christmas gig were the boss and Peter. So when Cass arrived soon after, I made a beeline for her, 'So glad you're here!' When we went to find a seat, Peter sat directly behind me at the next table with all the other senior clinicians. I suppose I was expected to join them, but I was far happier with Cass and the medics.

I started to feel more conscious of them over my shoulder as the night continued, and by the time the cheese platter arrived, I just wanted to go home. Then a wicked thought struck me: screw it, I'm probably leaving anyway, so I might as well have a laugh. 'Cass, quick, take a photo of me,' I said, giggling. I sweetly smiled at the camera, as I flipped a middle finger over my shoulder for the benefit of the top table. Childish I know, but I couldn't resist. Cass took the pic and we couldn't stop laughing. I sent it to Sam, and got the 'laugh out loud' emoji back. That was it. The party began and we were all up dancing around our table without a care in the world.

I managed to catch the ear of the longest serving, 'take no crap' civil servant in the med centre, when she joined our company on the dance floor. Having given her the short version of work events, she agreed to join me for the mediation on Monday. I doubt this was expected, as the two men were seated when I arrived, with one chair ready for me. They quickly pulled up a second chair for the receptionist to take notes and I proceeded to boss the meeting.

I had my questions prepared and all I needed to clarify was, 'Who is tasked with managing me?' Once it was confirmed that

Peter was appointed, I set about taking the path of least resistance myself. 'I now need to make a decision as to whether this role is still a fit for me,' I began, 'It was supposed to be a short-term measure on downsizing my practice, while I worked out the plan. So, I want to sleep on things and get back to you tomorrow.' 'Well it would be a shame if you left because you get on well and we really appreciate your work,' the boss added. 'I second that,' the receptionist said.

I was reassured that the boss was enough on side, that when he offered to write my exit report, I accepted. The next morning, I sent my resignation, suggesting that as I had planned to move on soon in any case, Peter may do better with a new team. Peter bought me a bottle of wine and a card. I accepted it, as I realised that as far as he was concerned, he had done nothing wrong. From a higher perspective, he has a point. We can all miss the mark when it comes to communication, and in our time working together; I believe Peter did his best to be supportive. Besides, I learned valuable lessons from the whole experience.

The best surprise though, was on my last day. At morning tea, we were joined by virtually the whole medical centre. There was standing room only for all the medics. I was impressed that they managed to get a collection together in a week, for a gift and card. It felt so genuine and I was touched by the gesture. Putting so much energy into this role, certainly felt appreciated by everyone else. The lesson for me was that with more discernment and better boundaries, I could ensure that the workload would be sustainable next time around.

When I reflect on the experience of meeting my Dad with dementia, the biggest surprise was his reduced emotional maturity. I could no longer have the same expectations in that domain. I was ready to meet him at his altered perception of the world, with missing information or regressed time orientation, but the change in personality was unexpected. Meeting him at his level of maturity took adjusting to, partly because it took some time to understand (he hid his temperament well). It would have been unfair for me, not to have met him where he was at. Also, when I did, things became much more fun. This applies more broadly to others in that it would be painful to expect something from someone that they don't have the map for, or the capacity to supply.

Meeting people where they're at, or in other words, learning the boundary of where I end and the other person begins, has been the best solution to challenging my co-dependent tendencies, because this defines the lines of responsibility. In a situation of a vulnerable adult, I would assume more responsibility in the relationship; but for someone who is simply behaving irresponsibly, boundaries and limits need to be set. Whilst co-dependent behaviour can be seen as shouldering the responsibility of others, it also prevents the co-dependent from taking full responsibility for their own life.

This flip was the big wake up for me. That in being other centred, I was running away from taking full responsibility for my best life. I couldn't deny it; I took an honest look at my life and it was a bit of a mess. Sure, I had helped my folks in a vulnerable situation and would do that again 100 times over; but there I was, weeks after returning home, averaging 3 hours sleep a night for thinking about their problems. I hadn't even unpacked my bags from the trip, let alone put my business downsize in order; for distractions ranging from holidays away, working crazy hours or getting over involved in other people's problems.

In accepting that having expectations of others out of line with their capacity is futile and best not taken personally, I've become more forgiving of others and myself. I've had a lifetime of weak boundaries and was suffering the consequences at ever increasing levels of pain. There may have been merit and growth in challenging the boss' call or establishing boundaries with my newly appointed line manager. I agreed that the challenge, was a bit of a stretch at that time. Instead of fighting, I decided to yield. To let this one go, reclaim responsibly for my life and my boundaries moving forward. At Sam's suggestion, I took some time off.

I once recounted to Mum how amazing Karen was for asking after us whilst away on holidays. She was also contacting insurers to sort her own mum's roof repair from storm damage. Mum replied that she heard that Karen loves doing it, so her family let her get on with it. 'I'm not sure that's the case, and pretty sure that no-one loves doing that on their holidays Mum.' If I lived in Australia, I may have arrived as the lead of helping family. I hope that I'd do it gladly and without resentment. I might have been like Karen, the shepherd who puts her staff in the ground and all would round up. But if I'm to honour my own responsibilities, I have to accept that there are physical and financial limits to what I could do from the UK.

What I can do is inspire others to action, in a way that states my limits and gives people a choice, without investment or judgement on my part.

When I get into judging a person or a situation, I remember that my world is a map, not the territory. That I'm only seeing part of that person's life through my own limited understanding. To judge their behaviour would be, as the Talmud put it:

To project my view of *'them as I am,'* rather than *'as they really are.'*

Instead I choose to look at everyone as both limited in nature as fellow humans and unlimited as we all have infinite potential. This doesn't mean that I condone selfish or disrespectful behaviour, but I lose the need to judge or call it out. There is nothing to judge, nothing to forgive, when we accept that we all sin differently. If everything that I see in the world is in my own mind map, then I might as well aim for world peace.

Without attaching to the issue, my response became like a game of chess or tennis. I passed over all the recent documents regarding Mum and Dad, informing my brothers and sister that I can't manage this any further from here. I would be on holidays for 10 days over Christmas without mobile signal. When the push back came in the form of excuses like, 'We're extremely busy', 'I have my own family to look after', 'I'll leave you to continue the excellent work that you are doing' etc, I put the ball back in their court. 'I've sent the documents to all of you and I trust that you will find a solution between you.'

What followed was 10 days of bliss. I was lying on a shaded couch in sunny Fuerteventura and as my energy returned, sleep started normalising and my head cleared, the simplest thought occurred to me. I just need to stop doing stuff for stuff to stop landing with me. So when I returned home, I took a mental and physical step back, to allow others to continue to step in. Adam texted in response to my decision, 'At least you can't be seen as the overbearing one.' To love without attachment, I thought, is to watch and understand someone's pain without taking it on or trying to fix it. Then, signpost them, set challenges, and give them experiences so that they can find what they need.

I think that learning to temper a caretaking tendency might be quite common in caring professions, as they're the most likely to self-select for these roles. This may in part account for the high rate of burnout in healthcare. With new insight, I now operate more as a coach than a therapist. After listening and checking that my understanding is correct, I offer my assessment. 'This is the situation as I see it. Here are your options, what do you choose?'

Now when I help others, it's a conscious decision, coming from a much more mature and useful place. I discern whether I'm helping or enabling and from the broadest and highest perspective possible, I choose where my efforts are best spent for the greatest impact and what's most meaningful for me. Since I've committed to getting my house in order, I come from a space of compassionate detachment, both with patients and in my life relationships.

I took break for 3 months. I saw the current patients on my list and took no new work on so I could run one clinic a fortnight. We managed to live on less (for a time) more comfortably than I expected and this allowed me to simplify things and look to what's most important. It was great to put the pause button on life. I was able to have the space and breath to really bed in my habits of self-care; getting my house in good order. Sam was clever to suggest this break, as I actually experienced a new way of being and was determined not to go back to that crazy old lifestyle.

With the luxury of time, I was really able to set my intention for how I wanted to serve. I applied for and landed a part time role at the army base, located just minutes from home. I found much scope to be an advocate for the personnel. There was a full-time role available but I also sensed that unless I spent some time in private practice, with the team of my choosing, I would miss the freedom and opportunities for growth. So, after a couple of coffee catch ups, I took up 2 days a week back at Dr Speight's place in Leeds.

For the first time in my career, I wasn't reaching out for bigger and better, but actually going for known entities. Instead of running away from a poor system, I made a conscious move toward these roles; choosing the best of both worlds. I would be fulfilled meeting these roles on my terms, and hopefully for the long term.

There are possible changes to the army role in line with cost cutting on the horizon. If implemented, this will see the scope and admin load of my role extended. We would also share premises with the NHS. Whilst I may not be a fan of these changes, I accept that these decisions are above my pay grade. I intend to continue to do the best with what I have and focus on what I can influence in the present.

Returning to Martyn's clinic felt like coming home. It's a family business run by his wife, Lisa and himself. Martyn's sister Sally, covers reception, so it was like being back amongst old friends. As a family concern, there is so much care and all are in alignment with taking a stand for quality care. Martyn is passionate about good medicine and as I told him, 'You're here to keep me sane.' Although I suspect we drive Lisa and Sally insane at times, with our rants about healthcare politics over lunchbreaks. Being part of both teams again, has made me appreciate them even more and from a new perspective. As TS Elliot said,

"At the end of all our exploring will be to arrive where we started and know the place for the first time."

I saw things steadily fall into place for Mum too. Her angiogram came back clear and so cardiac was being monitored under meds. Her appointment with a psychologist came through and she was getting on well with her. We managed to downsize the car so that we freed up some cash and it was under the threshold value for repossession. On communicating with the bank, an independent financial counsellor was appointed to advocate on Mum's behalf and would negotiate an affordable payment plan. Daniela helped Mum successfully apply for financial hardship which meant that care home respite for Dad was heavily subsidised and their rental lease was complete now, so options were opening up.

Their place on the wait list for the highest-level care plan had come through, so a case manager was appointed. She authorised someone to mow the lawn, added another half day a week of in-home care cover and up to 2 half days a week of activities out for Dad. Two weeks respite in a care home was being arranged.

'The real estate called in today to let me know that the owner has put the house on the market,' Mum began, 'Although they don't have a buyer yet, they thought it best to let us know so that we can be on the lookout for somewhere else.' The new owner might want an ongoing tenant, but if not, they promised to help them find a place. 'Dad is due in for 2 weeks respite next week, but I might ask them to take him in for a month.' 'I think that's a good idea,' I replied, 'It'll give you time to pack some things and look at your options.

'You know, the old Dad comes back now and then,' Mum commented, the day after dropping him off to the care home. He said, to her on their way there, 'Don't visit too often because it's far for you to travel and it's not good for you.' 'I almost cried' Mum confessed.

It reminded me of the morning that the airport shuttle was picking me up from Mum and Dad's house last year. I expected Dad to wave from his armchair, as I had it in my mind, that he was too much in his own world, transfixed on the telly, to be bothered with goodbyes. But the moment I picked up my bags to load them onto the bus, he sprung up and followed me out. Even then, because I had already framed him as that stranger, incapable of empathy, I reasoned that he cared for me in a superficial kind of way. I gave him a huge hug, to give him the experience, but like an actress, I didn't let myself feel it. If anyone in that moment was void of empathy, it was me. I had taken to black and white thinking as a coping mechanism. That the Dad, as we knew it was gone. Gone is easier to cope with than comes and goes. The greys are closer to truth, but harder to appreciate and much more painful to deal with. If I had my time again in that moment, I would have wanted to hold onto him for an eternity. Embracing and feeling the love, and appreciation to receive this precious rare, perhaps final appearance. I wish that I was ready to receive it at the time, but I accept that I was processing so much and holding so much together. I just wasn't there yet. But I am now, and I can still feel it.

'It's so quiet here in the house and I'm surprised to find that I actually missed him last night.' continued Mum. 'Of course you will', I replied, 'you've shared a lifetime with him.' A few days later, a new insight landed for Mum. More than missing the memory of her husband, she realised how much she missed her life. This landed after a few days of being free of the smell, the interrupted sleep, the constant running around picking things up, cooking, cleaning, giving repeated instructions, which were ignored, argued with, or forgotten. His repeated questions, paranoia and aggression. Her being confined to the house much of the time. After a few days of peace, she realised that she couldn't go back to that life.

'It's better to be honest and decide,' I affirmed, 'rather than push on until it falls apart and it becomes an emergency for your health or his, or both.' Even though she knew, I reminded her out loud, that things would only get tougher as his abilities decline. 'That's just it ' she said, 'all I was doing was watching him slowly get worse in that chair and I couldn't do anything. I'd ask him to move, try to motivate him, I'd cry, I'd nag, I'd not nag, and nothing I said or do could make him move.' 'He's more likely to respond to the carers,' I reassured her. 'Whatever I said he wouldn't remember anyway. I just felt so helpless....' I had heard enough to know that she was sure. 'Then it's simple,' I replied. 'We don't have to weigh up 2 options. Taking him back out is not an option. It's just a matter of downsizing your kit and finding an affordable place for you to live.' After speaking to Daniela, Mum learned that she can have 63 days respite before her carers allowance would be discontinued. In that time, she can get things in order and would share the news with the rest of the family at a time of her choosing.

Just for the finality of it, I shed a few tears that evening. In typical Sam fashion, he asked whether the tears were for Dad or myself. I've learned not to react to these questions, as I think we'll always have a different view on grieving. I asked him instead, to just let me move through it in my own way. One thing that helped me move through it more quickly, was looking up Dad's new home online. It was the most stunning conversion of an old convent. The architecture and high ceilings had a light and airy feel. It was spotless but not clinical looking, the design of the space, the views of the boat jetty, the gardens, patio areas, rooms and communal areas were arranged so tastefully. I was moved to the point of welling up when I read that they organise activities to nurture the social, lifestyle and spiritual health of their residents. They were dementia friendly and could handle his medical needs including the stoma care. They were in the catchment of the major hospital. No one wanted this situation, but in terms of responding to it, this is the best outcome that we could have hoped for.

Sam suggested that just in case Mum received any argument from family, or in case she suffered any doubts, that I express how I feel in a note. I wrote an email to both Mum and Daniela summarising the journey and reaffirming how I'm in support of her decision. The burden of a decision halved, by both of us agreeing. I asked her to keep a copy with her, to maintain perspective on her reasons and to be under no mistake about my view.

'....Putting Dad into respite has allowed Mum to reflect on just how difficult things have been and that despite getting services in, that it's unmanageable for her to sustain. Whilst I sense from talking to her yesterday, that she might feel a little defeated in this reflection; I would say that it's not a failure at all, but a wise acceptance of the human limitations of one person, versus a team of professional carers. I think that Mum wouldn't even discuss the option of a care home for so long, because she's very determined and cares deeply for Dad. I actually see it as a success that she has transitioned Dad into care, in a well-planned and managed way. She's selected an exceptional location and, timing this to be long term now, means that Dad can settle into life in the care home without interruption. As you know, those with Alzheimer's do best with routine. I'm pleased that Mum has her clarity on this, as it's the best thing for her health and wellbeing ....' This correspondence also allowed me to give thanks for Daniela's hard work, skill, diligence, organisation, persistence and compassion. That it has made such a difference to our lives.

The passage was timely, as Mum received a fair bit of flak from several family members when she shared her decision. Dad's sister (a classic co-dependent type, interestingly) said, 'If you leave him in that place, you may as well give him a bag of pills.' Mum responded with clarity and without allowing such accusations to affect her. 'I've been his carer since the cancer and I wish I could continue, but I simply can't. He's my husband, who I love, and I did a lot of soul searching, before I finally decided that this is the best thing for him. He'll be well cared for and safe.' I shared with Mum that I think people often have very strong reactions to nursing homes, because they're looking at themselves in the situation, instead of seeing it from the perspective and needs of the residents. Most also have a poor understanding of the pathway of the disease, as if Alzheimer's is just about forgetting things, like what you had for breakfast or where you placed your keys. They're not understanding how unwell he is medically and the level of care that he needs. There's a reason he was awarded the top level of care on his plan.

'Also, I think that part of the problem is that Dad is very good at hiding how affected he is.' I added. 'He so is!' Mum agreed,

'He changes completely for visitors and being intelligent, can give off the impression that he's holding it all together.' 'Yeah, for sure, I said, 'that's their perspective, from time spent in a brief social situation, in casual conversation. They're not seeing all of the picture.' I reminded her that it took me a few days of living in the house to understand. 'So, they may never understand. If you ask Dad, he'll probably always say that he's fine and doesn't need to be there.'

Putting on that we 'have it all together' is a strategy that we all employ to some extent (both consciously and unconsciously). Dad was agreeing to being in the care home because of his view that Mum wasn't coping. 'It's really for her not me,' he said to the carers the week before moving in. I suggested that if going along with him in his perception bolsters his confidence, then that's not a bad thing. In an environment that's more stable and less challenging, he can thrive by feeling confident. 'It's just a matter of whether you can cope with the family judging you,' I cautioned. To my relief, she replied, 'Ah, I don't give a fuck about that.' I laughed and hoped that this stayed the case.

'They're being dramatic. It's not the end of his life, he's not in a prison,' I said, still laughing because I've only heard my Mum swear a handful of times in my life. 'Outings are organised twice a week and I'm planning to take him out for a meal each week. I actually look forward to seeing him now and have given him more kisses and hugs than I have in a long while,' Mum smiled, 'I can authorise Seth and a couple of nominated cousins to have permission to take him out too.' 'There you go, he's going to have a better social life than me.' I smiled back.

Seth and Alex stepped in to help Mum downsize and move into her new apartment. Finding her own place and moving on with her life must be such a difficult thing for Mum to do after over 40 years of marriage to the love of her life. Being on your own after someone has passed away is one thing, but to do so when they're still alive must feel both strange and painful.

Chapter 14

The final voyage

"There are only two ways to live your life. One as though nothing is a miracle. The other as if everything is."

Albert Einstein.

For the first 4 decades of my life, I took myself down a road of putting everyone else first, thinking that this was the way to love. Service above self – just like my Dad, or so I thought. Eventually, I was serving from an empty cup and this co-dependent form of love helped no-one. I then took lessons from Mum's example in finding a way to serve, not through a self-sacrificial type of martyrdom, but wisely, from a place of highest self. Accepting limits and setting boundaries actually takes more humility.

Other experiences have taught me the value of forgiveness for myself and others. To let things be, without taking it personally or needing to fix. If my younger self were a close friend, I could easily forgive her as she knew no different, but moving forward

I would encourage her to commit the rest of her life to looking after herself.

I keep my house in order by maintaining daily rituals that lift my wellbeing. All the things that we advise those with chronic pain to do. Sustain a clean diet, some daily form of exercise, be it yoga, running or strength work, sleep hygiene, journaling, mediation and downtime. I'm not perfect at it, but I'm never far away from the habits as a priority.

I really noticed the effect on my boundaries the first time that I fell out of my routine. I stayed up a couple of hours later than usual, to indulge in unproductive web surfing on my phone. The lack of sleep (and screen light) fell in time with my intermittent fasting routine, and the next morning, I watched myself as a result, revert to the way that I used to practice. Coming from a depleted space I once again, lacked the discernment between helping and enabling. Over-giving and taking more responsibility than I should in the sessions, left me running over time and feeling even more drained. However, I now know a different way of being, so I avoided that downward spiral by quickly returning to my habits of self-care.

I reflected from that experience, to remember that from a full cup, we can serve others far more wisely.

Sam lives his life with such playfulness that it's contagious. We recently bought a campervan and regularly hike out in nature to appreciate the pauses in life, the spaces in between. His example has taught me to embrace life lightly and accept that all types of maps belong in the world. No traits are inherently good or bad and all experiences instruct as lessons.

The very process of writing this book has been a huge source of growth for me. I've been able to express my needs and feelings. To reflect and learn the lessons more deeply. Then reflect some more and tell a deeper truth. I've been able to step back from my life and surrender it all with a renewed perspective and purpose. It's brought me peace and clarity.

Tomorrow I turn 42. That's 19 years since I received my physio registration papers with my hands trembling. I remember listening to Dr Mark Jones lecture on the acquisition of expertise, citing sources that it takes 10,000 hours of quality practice or roughly 10 years. I felt a background sense of unease at my 9-year point, as I wondered whether I'll have done enough to get there. Yet I couldn't tell you if the 10-year date was a Tuesday, or even on which month it fell. I guess I had a beginner's mindset by then and the question of whether, 'I was there yet?' wasn't so relevant.

The human qualities required of an expert, are the very same that I asked myself about 9 years ago, when I learned of Dad's Leukaemia diagnosis. I asked myself whether I could show up as that person my Dad taught me to be. In a year from now, would I ask myself whether my life is an example of the lessons of his legacy? I realise now, that I've always been that person. Not in a perfect way, but no one is. More than learning from the person that he modelled, I'm the person that I am and that's enough. Dad I thank you for every lesson you taught me and the many more to come.

Since waking up from my car crash, I've asked myself deeper questions of a spiritual nature. I read a fascinating book named 'Proof of Heaven.' It was written by neurosurgeon, Dr Ebden Alexander [1]. Whilst suffering total, (but temporary) cortical brain damage, Ebden experienced a very vivid spiritual experience. He explained it in the following way: We know that the brain acts as a filter. Approximately 11 million bits of information hit the senses each second, but the limit of our processing capacity is thought to be 120 bits. So, the brain needs to narrow our consciousness, otherwise we wouldn't be able to function in the world. From his near-death experience, Dr Alexander changed his view from the brain being the seat of consciousness, to the spiritual dimension existing outside ourselves. He posits instead, that the human brain tends to filter out spiritual states. This has provided some comfort to me with regards Dad's condition. The picture of what is presenting in the physical world with respect to Dad's decline, may be entirely different to what he might be experiencing spiritually.

Practices recommended to raise one's spiritual consciousness include cultivating a level of detachment, as an observer of the material world. Looking at the world anew through the innocent eyes of a child and staying in the moment. I see Alzheimer's returning my Dad to that more innocent, present, childlike state. If I look past the limitations of my worldview and beyond what is presenting physically, I can choose to see the soul that is untouched by the changes in his body and brain. A soul that is ascending and perhaps preparing Dad for the final chapter of his life, to return to a higher power [3].

When I practice raising my consciousness, I meet life where it is, without evaluating from my limited perspective, allowing me to accept things as they are. I can let go of trying to control or steer situations to bend to my will and instead surrender to a higher power that understands it from all perspectives. I'm humble enough to know that it's not for me to know why, or how things should be, all I need to do is keep asking, 'How might I best serve.'

Sam and I went on a coastal walk during one of our recent trips to south-west Scotland. From the campsite, we followed a path signposted to St Ninian's cave. Despite the sunshine, the wind howled up so strongly that I soon lost too much heat. We sat on a beach and he wrapped me up until the resultant fatigue and ear pain passed. Sitting there, shielded from the wind, Sam and I picked out the prettiest pebble that we could find and with it still in my hand, we headed off to explore the cave. At its entrance, we learned of this cave's religious significance. Thought to be the retreat of Scotland's first saint, St Ninian used this secluded spot as a place of solitude and prayer in the late AD 300s.

Subsequently, pilgrims from the land and sea sheltered there, to give thanks for their safe harbour and pray for their ongoing journey. It remains a site for religious pilgrims to this day. In this sacred space, I placed the pebble on a ledge and prayed silently for Dad. There was nothing that I needed in my life and I had come to accept his condition and his journey. What I did ask for, as I turned to look out over the Irish sea to views of England and the Isle of Man, was that his voyage of ascent, be as smooth sailing as possible.

May the road rise up to meet you.
May the wind be always at your back.
May the sun shine warm upon your face;
the rains fall soft upon your fields
and until we meet again,
may God hold you in the palm of His hand.

Irish Proverb.

Further Reading

1. Alexander, E. (2012). Proof of Heaven: A Neurosurgeon's Journey into the Afterlife. London: Piatkus.

2. Covey, S. (1989). The Seven Habits of Highly Effective People. New York: Simon and Schuster.

3. Hyland-Rogers, L. Dementia from a Spiritual Perspective. Blog: http://symphonyofsoul.org/alzheimer%E2%80%99s-and-dementia-a-spiritual-perspective/

4. James, O. (2008). Contented Dementia. London: Vermillion.

5. Jones, M. (2019). Clinical Reasoning in Musculoskeletal Practice. London: Elsevier.

Printed in Poland
by Amazon Fulfillment
Poland Sp. z o.o., Wrocław

50112260R00132